PRAISE FO.

BUILD YOUR BRAND LIKE YOU GIVE A SHIT

"In the always-on economy, brand authenticity matters more than ever. Bobby's *BYBLYGaS* is a blueprint for understanding why you get out of bed in the morning and how to activate brand loyalty based on your true self.

—**Alexei Yukna,** veteran advertising and marketing technology executive

"When it comes to building a brand, Bobby doesn't beat around the bush. As a brand clarity expert who has been in the business for over two decades helping his clients clarify their brands, Bobby keeps it fucking real. By focusing on the core message, he taps into the heart and soul of a brand. In his new book, he brings the same authenticity, audacity, and personality onto the page. From success stories to unforeseeable mistakes, Bobby puts everything on the line because his brand is his reputation. His writing is as authoritative as it is informative. If you give a shit about building your brand, this book is for you."

—**Donny Truong,** Director of Design & Web Services, Antonin Scalia Law School, George Mason University, author of Vietnamese Typography & Professional Web Typography

"Bobby's been successfully helping brands for over 20 years but even more impressive is his ability to live out his teachings. If you work with him or subscribe to his content you know he leads by word and example."

—**Ozzy Torres,** Marketing Manager at CloseKnit

"In typical Bobby G form, he gets in your face about your brand. He takes us all the way to the root of our brands - our core values. Bobby is our big brother loving us enough to tell us the truth. The truth is that people who give a sh!t about their brands will reveal their potential in this milk toast market. Authenticity is what it's all about; Bobby lives it in our face in Build Your Brand. Read this book, then build your brand."

—**Jason Blumer,** CPA, CEO of Blumer CPAs, CEO of Thriveal Network, Consultant and Advisor to agencies that want to scale

"Bob is the ultimate brand pro. Knowing him for several years, it has been amazing to watch him refine and perfect his craft. He is one of the deepest thinkers I know. Bob is firm in his convictions and will always give it to you straight. Anyone looking to build or improve their brand will benefit from this book."

—**Chris Feroli,** VP Sales Dynamic Yield

— BUILD YOUR BRAND

LIKE YOU GIVE A SH!T

Embrace your purpose
and unleash your potential

BY BOBBY GILLESPIE

propr

Cover deisgn by Faceout Studio, Amanda Hudson
Interior design by Faceout Studio, Paul Nielsen

This interior was desigend using Arno Pro and Berthold Akzidenz Grotesk.

The advice and strategies found within may not be suitable for every
situation. This work is sold with the understanding that neither the author
nor the publisher is held responsible for the results accrued from the advice
in this book.

Published by ProprBooks.com

Library of Congress Control Number: 2022913361

ISBN:
979-8-218-01713-2 (hardcopy print),
979-8-218-03260-9 (softcover)
979-8-218-02548-9 (ebook)

Summary

Your brand is not your logo; it is your reputation. Everything you say,
post, and publish reflects your brand; that's why you must give a shit about
your brand. You can reach your potential by leading with authenticity and
embracing your purpose.

First edition.

Für Elise, Jane & Emmet

CONTENTS

INTRODUCTION

Maybe you've heard the old story about the man who approached Michelangelo to praise him for his marble statue of David.

"Sir," he said, "how in God's name could you have created such a masterpiece from a crude slab of marble?"

And, as the story goes, the famed Renaissance artist turned to the man, gave him a wry smile, and replied, "Oh, it was very easy. I simply chipped away at the stone that didn't look like David."

I get chills when I think about that story because that's the reality of brand right there! Who you are, what you stand for, what you're all about it, it's right there—you just have to extract it. Unfortunately, it's a task that seems impossible, and that's why so many brands come off like cold, hard, shapeless slabs of stone.

So, Dear Reader, the question is, "What's holding you back from revealing your brand's very own David?"

Maybe the fact that it's hard as hell. I've been in this business for more than twenty years, and as a brand clarity expert, I've helped dozens of companies clarify their brands. Even so, I get a lot of resistance from clients who don't feel like they need to work on their branding.

"Oh, we know who we are," they say.

"Okay, then, tell me," I reply. "Tell me what really matters to your company. Tell me who your customers are. Tell me what really matters to them. Tell me why you do what you do and for whom."

And this is usually followed by a long pause,

because they just can't articulate their brand in a clear, concise manner.

Look, we all know damn well Michelangelo didn't just chip away the extra bits of stone and "uncover" David in that slab of marble. He worked like hell to perfect his craft, and through many years of training and apprenticeship, he eventually acquired the expertise to painstakingly carve the image of David using precise tools and a lot of skill. That's why most of us aren't sculpting our own marble masterpieces. For whatever reason, we aren't committed to what it takes to create our own masterpiece.

And, by the way, that's exactly why a lot of people haven't really defined their brand yet. Some aren't willing to do the hard work, or they're downright terrified, or maybe they don't even know where to start. It's not easy having to chip away at your own mess. Others only care about money or status, and some resist admitting that they lack clarity about their brand because they're afraid it will make them look incompetent, unprofessional, or stupid.

But if you don't clarify who you are, what you stand for, and what you really give a shit about, then how do you know if you're doing the right thing? What happens when you're not around and someone has to make a critical decision in your place? What message are you putting out into the world about your company? How the hell do you hire the right people?

When you think about it, marketing is just telling the world who you are. In a very real sense, the message you put out *is* marketing. How it's interpreted, and how it makes people feel, that's your brand. Both contribute to your reputation. So, what are you telling the world about yourself? And are you telling honest stories? People have gotten super cynical about "brand values" because so many of the messages are bullshit that don't reflect how leaders actually behave.

But when you know who you are, when you are authentic, then you can market with confidence because you know you're sending the right message to the right people in the right voice. And when your brand is real and authentic, you eliminate all competition, because no one can compete with you on being you.

On the other hand, when you're just trying to compete on products, services, ingredients, or features, you're fighting on a level playing field, commoditizing yourself. Someone will come along and offer a comparable product that is better, cheaper, and faster. That makes it a race to the bottom.

More than ever, people want to patronize brands that they relate to. They want to know that you're real human beings who stand for something and give a damn, and they're willing to pay more to companies that are likable and relatable. Globally, 94 percent of consumers say it's important that the companies they engage with have a strong purpose.[1]

In my humble opinion, your marketing should be all about communicating and connecting authentically. Yeah, you can try to fake it. Lots of brands do.

1   https://www.forbes.com/sites/afdhelaziz/2020/06/17/global-study-reveals-consumers-are-four-to-six-times-more-likely-to-purchase-protect-and-champion-purpose-driven-companies/

Ironically, it's incredibly expensive and resource-draining to fake it. Sooner or later, people will see through it, and when they do, your reputation will take a nosedive.

So, here's a wild idea. Why not compete, communicate, and connect in an authentic way? Why not have values and actually embody those values in everything you do? Why not expose the real David within the slab of marble that is your brand, and make a difference? Why not stop trying gimmicks, treating people like crap, or throwing shit at the wall and hoping it'll stick, and move the needle?

I'm convinced there's a better way to hire people, unify your team, work with clients, connect and work with your target audience, and solidify your authority and legacy—a way that minimizes waste and maximizes impact. And it's all about being a decent fucking human being.

Who the Hell Are You?

A few years ago, I had dinner with a good friend who was just about to move to Texas. It was sort of a farewell dinner, and as we swapped stories, he asked me if I knew that his mom ran a design agency.

"She works hard, man. She works hard. But so many times, when she finally presents to a client, they just complain and derail the whole project," he said. "All of those hours of hard work just to have a client look at the results for a few seconds and say, 'Eh, I don't like it.' She's so damned frustrated and exhausted with clients."

We've all been there, haven't we? All of your hard work and effort getting dismissed within seconds when you finally present it. It's incredibly stressful, and quite frankly, it sucks.

In a former life, I was the creative director of an e-commerce agency. While there, I was in charge of a project for a client who sold expensive espresso machines. Our job was to redesign their enterprise website, so we talked with the CEO about the business case, what they did, their average order value, and so on. They were trying to improve the marketability of the website in order to drive more traffic, engagement, and generate more conversions.

We looked at the information architecture, structure, navigation, and site map of the existing website, then we analyzed the user experience. All of this went fine, but when we got on the phone to discuss the website's design, the CEO's wife joined us on the call. At no point had she been identified as a decision-maker (or even a decision influencer) in the organization, so her participation was confusing. What we didn't know at the time was that she had designed the existing website herself.

During the call, we proposed some significant design changes to the website. We weren't particularly critical of the existing interface design, but we recommended a new approach. The owner, who had thus far been easy to work with, suddenly became contentious to even our most reasonable suggestions. More than that, he seemed to take our suggestions as a personal attack. We were shocked at the hostility. He'd hired us to do exactly what we were doing. Why was he so upset that we were recommending design changes to the website?

As soon as we got off the phone, the CEO contacted the owner of our agency and fired us. His wife, it turned out, was rather sensitive about her website design, and our recommendations had hurt her feelings. That wasn't our intention, of course. We were simply trying to do our job.

I came away from that meeting frustrated as hell, but instead of losing my shit, I sat down with my team and said, "Okay, what do we have to do to prevent this from ever happening again?"

Our tendency in situations like this is to complain about the client. We say things like, "What the hell was wrong with that idiot? What a jerk!" But what if we made it not about their ego, their foibles, or their personal preferences. What if we made it about what is best for our clients and their brands?

That's what I decided to do. I said, "We need a new intake process that ensures we always know exactly who we're working for from the beginning. That way we will always know that we're doing what's best for the brand and for the customer."

So, I explored ways to improve our processes, eliminating uncertainty, insecurity, whims, and ego, and preventing buyer's remorse. I shifted my focus to the client's brand and their customers, and I discovered that we could take a radically different approach, a more authentic brand-focused approach that enabled us to deliver something that felt right to every client we worked with.

That meant admitting to myself, "Hey, Bob, this isn't about what you like or want. This is about knowing for sure what's best for the client's brand and for their customers so you know you're not delivering something that they don't need."

In order to do that, I had to develop a process for extracting the foundational elements of a brand—starting with the non-negotiable core values. And what did I discover? That to understand a brand, you have to get to the heart and soul of what they truly stand for and care the most about—their core message, their big idea. When you can clarify these things, you can begin to contextualize what is appropriate for a client in terms of your words, image, tone, voice, and so on.

It also helps you understand their customers: who they are, what they care about, what channels they're on, what their pains and gains are, and what they truly care about and find relatable to their brand.

By starting with the core values of a brand—the heart and soul of the brand—we were able to gain clarity and confidence about the decisions we made for our clients, and that put an end to projects getting derailed after countless hours of hard work.

Ten years after this discovery, I wonder how any agency can operate without this critical information.

Who the Hell Am I?

The same clarity that we sought about our clients, we also had to seek for ourselves. When you understand the authentic core values of your brand, then you can make decisions on a rock-solid foundation. This gives leaders incredible confidence in their decision-making because they know what's best for their company. They know what's best for their customers. They know how to hire. They know who they are! It's no longer about ego, or insecurities, or uncertainties, so you can start unleashing your potential and building your reputation.

So, when my friend was lamenting the frustrations of his mother's graphic design agency, and the string of client derailments that wasted so much of her time and resources, I responded very simply, "I no longer have to worry about that. I've taken client rejection out of the equation."

"How do you do that?" he asked, staring at me in amazement (and confusion).

"Well, you don't start with implementation," I explained. "You don't say, 'We just need to do a better job on what we deliver.' Nope, by then it's too late. You start with understanding your brand—that means your authentic values, message, and personality—laying that foundation and then building everything on top of it, including the clients you work with."

Have you ever noticed how some people don't worry about their legacy until they're on the verge of death? Think about those rich old guys who have spent their whole lives just looking out for number one. After forty or fifty years as cutthroat businessmen, they get a few years from death, and suddenly they start becoming philanthropic, suddenly they become generous. Suddenly, they want to "leave a lasting legacy" by giving money to a public park or a college fund. It's too late. The reputation they'll die with is the reputation they've built—and earned.

The same goes for your brand. Your brand is your reputation. You're not going to throw some money into building a public park and suddenly undo a bad reputation.

So, who the hell are you as a brand? What do you stand for? What do you really give a shit about? What is the work of art hidden inside all of that shapeless rock? When you gain clarity about that, you'll be able to make decisions with incredible confidence and power, and that's the game-changer right there. And maybe, just maybe, you'll be a better human being for it.

PART ONE

Be Yourself *and* Be Great at Business

CHAPTER ONE

Are You Faking It?

"Fake it until you make it."

What terrible advice. Where the hell did this horrible saying come from, and why is it so ingrained into our business culture? It encourages people to be disingenuous, inauthentic, and phony.

So here's what I think. Granted, I'm a contrarian by nature, so I tend to question everything, and I despise trends. Still, I think it's perfectly okay to admit you don't know everything, as long as you're willing to learn more about what you don't know.

When I first started in business, like a lot of newbies, I had to do whatever I could do to bring in money. My dream was to create my own agency— not a one-person freelancer business but a real, live design agency. However, as I said, I had to bring in money, so when I got the opportunity to do some short-term work for a big agency, I went for it.

During a discovery call, they asked me if I had ever designed an iOS app. Did I fake it until I made it? Did I lie and say, "Oh, of course I've designed iOS apps! You bet!" That's what a lot of people would have done. It's what our business culture would recommend: "Just tell them whatever they want to hear. You can figure out what you don't know later."

Nope, not this trend-hating contrarian. Instead, I told the truth. "No, I've never designed an iOS app, but I can't wait to learn."

What would have happened if I'd lied and said yes? Well, the company that hired me would have assumed I already knew everything I needed to know, and it would have been on me to deliver something I knew I couldn't deliver. Consequently, it would have required a lot of extra work on my part before I could deliver what I'd promised, and all of that additional time would have been uncompensated. Ultimately, it would have been incredibly frustrating for me, for the agency, and for their client, as I took far longer to deliver a subpar product. All because I was faking it. But this is what we do. Despite the risk to our brand and our reputation, we fake it.

Instead, as I said, I took a different approach. I told them honestly that I'd never designed an iOS app but was excited to learn how. You might expect them to respond to such honesty by showing me the door. "Well, if you've never done it, then you're not the right person for the job."

Instead, they responded to my honest enthusiasm with, "That's fine. We'll help you through it."

In the end, we wound up collaborating on the app design. They helped me learn what I needed to know and showed me where to focus my energy. The project was very successful, and along the way, I created a great relationship with both the agency and their client.

And we achieved all of this *because* I didn't fake it.

No matter what product or service you provide, you create a stronger and more meaningful relationship with clients and their customers when you don't lay a foundation of lying, because you'll never have to worry about losing their trust when the lie is exposed. You'll never have to hear them say things like, "You told us you could create an iOS app, but what you've delivered is unimpressive and took too long to complete. We are disappointed in your results, and quite frankly, we feel conned."

Is that how you want people to react to your hard work? Is that the reputation you want to build? Do you want to be known as a bullshitter? If you're okay with that, then you should probably drop this book right now. Give it to someone else, because it won't do you any good.

What Is Good Enough?

"That's good enough." It's something we say a lot in my industry. When someone designs a mediocre website for a client, they'll justify it by saying, "Hey, it's good enough. What does a website cost anyway? We're not creating the Biltmore Estate or the Winchester Mansion here! It's the website equivalent of a modest suburban home. It's good enough!"

I'm sure a similar sentiment plagues most industries. "Good enough" tends to be the benchmark for a lot of companies creating a variety of products and services, but what does it mean? What do we mean when we say, "It's good enough?"

When you're building and marketing a brand, you're essentially playing an infinite game, because it has no finish line. While you have milestones, goals, and successes along the way, ultimately there's no intended completion date. You want to play well and stay in the game, competing for as long as possible. You don't build a brand, put it on a shelf, and say, "We're done. We built it. It's complete." No, you keep working on it, making it better and better for as long as you can (as good as you can).

In that sense, "good enough" should mean getting the most return for your efforts by allocating your limited resources to things that will bring measurable, quality returns that contribute to the infinite mission at that specific time. Even if you're only, metaphorically speaking, building modest single-family suburban homes, you should be putting your heart and soul into them for the people who will use them. It should be a quality effort, because quality begets quality. If you put your heart and soul into something, you're more likely to get a heartfelt response from the clients you serve. Plus, the feeling of ownership ensures people will care.

And if you fail along the way, you don't cover it up or lie about it. You learn from it. Seen that way, a mistake isn't something to bury in the backyard. Perfect doesn't really exist anyway, and if you pursue perfection, you're only going to end up with procrastination and paralysis.

As I tell my team members, "If you make a mistake while trying to do the right thing, be honest about it and move as quickly as you can to fix, and make it a learning experience. As long as you're not lazy, rushing, or sloppy, I won't hold it against you."

That kind of attitude creates a culture where people feel empowered and care about what they're doing. They own their mistakes because they're trying to do the right thing and they have the breathing room to correct mistakes without getting publicly flogged.

Many of the clients we work with are just starting to market themselves. They've had some success, but they've hit a ceiling as they attempt to scale. We put them through our Brand Clarity Workshop and help them identify and clarify who they are, who their customers are, and what matters to them. Then we redesign their website, and activate them for enthusiastic growth.

It would be a mistake for them to say at that point (as they sometimes do), "Well, we're done. We built our brand!" In reality, they're just getting started.

You have to live in your brand! You should be constantly working on it, creating a culture around your core values, hiring and competing around them, fanatically striving to live up to them. This requires dedication and giving a shit. For example, if kindness is part of your brand values, then you should be constantly working at embodying kindness in everything you do.

There are far too many organizations in the world espousing values that they don't fully embody. Since 1908, the Boy Scouts organization has championed twelve principles, called the "Scout Law," that all of their leaders are supposed to live by: "A Scout is trustworthy, loyal, helpful, friendly, courteous, kind, obedient, cheerful, thrifty, brave, clean, and reverent." Despite this, it was revealed in bankruptcy court in November 2020 that 92,700 sexual abuse claims have been filed against the Boy Scouts over the years, most of them accusations of abuse done by Scout leaders. According to attorney

Andrew Van Arsdale, sexual abuse in the Boy Scouts was "an unspoken norm."[2]

We've seen the same hypocrisy with churches and religious organizations who claim to be moral authorities even as they cover up widespread sexual abuse within their ranks. Priests and pastors decrying immorality from the pulpit, while the abusers among them are actively protected behind the scenes.

Hypocrisy. This is the central issue, and it absolutely infests the business world as well. On the one hand, you say you stand for something. You identify a set of values and pay lip service to them. On the other hand, those values aren't apparent or consistent in what you do. Even if you're not as blatant or as bad as the Boy Scouts, it's still a huge problem.

It's something you have to work at. Aligning every aspect of your company with your brand values is not a one-off project but part of the infinite game. Creating your core values and posting them online

2   https://time.com/5912452/boy-scouts-sexual-abuse-bankruptcy

or on the walls of your office is not the end, it's just the beginning. Now, you have to use them to guide everything you do.

Who you hire should be guided by your values, so the big-time sales guy on your team who is selfish, insecure, and bossy is conflicting with your values.

"Who cares? He's one of our top revenue generators," you might say.

If you keep a guy like that around then your core values are phony. Clearly, in practice, making money is your only value, and you'll do it by any means possible, even if you have to behave contrary to who you claim to be. That guy is making you money, but he's also decimating your reputation. What price are you willing to pay for short-term cash flow?

If you really cared about doing things the right way, he would be required to straighten up or take a hike. How can you expect a customer, vendor, or partner to take your values seriously if you overlook a team member's behavior simply because he brings in money? Just take the core values off your website. Pull the poster off your wall and throw it away, because you clearly don't believe them.

People see it. They see when you're a phony.

"Your core value is kindness, but your lead salesman is a notorious bully and a jerk."

And that's your reputation right there. That's what you're marketing, whether you realize it or not. Your message to your target audience is, "We believe our people can do whatever they want, as long as they bring in money." Put that on the poster and hang it on the wall. Try to compete and connect with people on that value, because practically speaking, that's who you are.

Only Better Is Better

I worked with a PR firm once who thought their major selling point was having forty employees. Their size was their selling point. Rather than focusing on what truly mattered to the customer, they thought like a lot of big companies: "Look at how many people are on our team! Clearly, we're the best."

Their assumption was that customers would see a bigger company as more stable, but in reality, when a customer deals with a big company, they mostly just feel depersonalized. They become a number. It's not a selling point. At best, it's a trade-off.

Stability isn't an asset anyway. It's just an impression or a perceived condition. Nevertheless, this particular PR firm put out press releases championing the size of their team anytime they hit what they believed to be a milestone.

"We now have thirty people on our team! We now have forty people on our team!"

I recall helping them put together a sales presentation pitch deck, and they wanted to lead with size. Finally, I said, "Why would anyone care about how many employees we have? Customers want a firm that's focused on relationships, innovation, and strategic communication, a firm that gets results! The only thing a bigger company gets them is a higher price, because you have higher overhead. Why would you lead with that? Bigger isn't better. Only better is better."

Unfortunately, there were just too many egos in the way to hear what I was saying.

It's as worthless as having pinball machines, a fancy sound system, and a bar in your office. It's as worthless as the $10,000 lease on your office space. None of these are selling points because none of them communicate value to the customer. They're just distractions.

Look, there's no shortcut to creating an honest, values-driven organization. It takes commitment and a lot of hard work. There's no "get rich quick" scheme for building an authentic brand. If you truly want to make an impact and change people's lives, you have to abandon the notion that there's some shortcut or hack that will get you there. Authentic, impactful brands require time, effort, and diligence.

You have to be excited and enthusiastic about what you're doing. Think of it this way. According to Daniel Coyle, author of *The Talent Code*, if you want to become a great guitar player, you need four things.

- First, you need access to a guitar.

- Second, you need to be enthusiastic about learning to play it.

- Third, you need to surround yourself with other people who like to play, who can push you, encourage you, and support you.

- Fourth, you need deep practice that is driven by a desire to get better.

As long as you have those four things, plus time, you will eventually gain expertise in playing guitar, and that, in turn, will transform enthusiasm into a real passion. The same goes for building and growing an authentic brand: you need access to opportunity, enthusiasm about what you're doing, the right environment of support and encouragement, and a desire to continually improve. With those elements, you will acquire the expertise you need, and your growth is practically inevitable.

From what I've seen, expertise is learned over time, and it gradually unleashes your passion. What you do is who you are. That's passion. It's not just a job. It's not just an interest. It's your life. Jimmy Hendrix wasn't just good at playing guitar. It became his identity, because it was his passion.

If you want to build and grow an authentic brand, realize you've got a long journey ahead of you, but it's a journey that never ends—and a journey that never ends. There's no destination. You're not creating a brand the way you create a monument. It goes on forever, so take the time to do it right. Hire and acquire people who are aligned with your brand values. Be careful who you surround yourself with and listen to. Some people don't have your best interests at heart. Avoid hacks and shortcuts, because even if they help you grow in the short term, they will have a negative impact on your reputation. And tell the truth, for fuck's sake!

Start out from day one building your brand the right way, defining and then embodying your values, so you don't lay down an unstable foundation of bullshit. No building can stand on a foundation of crap—it will eventually collapse. Hack and shortcuts don't contribute to years of consistent growth and impact—only a stellar reputation does that, so start building it now.

How do you do that? Well, shockingly, you do it by not focusing solely on "winning." Allow me to explain what I mean.

Chapter One Reflections:

- ► Your brand is your reputation, and your reputation is what you're marketing, whether you realize it or not.

- ► You create a stronger and more meaningful relationship with clients and their customers when you don't lay a foundation of bullshit (and you'll never have to worry about losing their trust when the bullshit is exposed).

- ► If you fail along the way, don't cover it up or lie about it. Learn from it.

- ► You don't build a brand, put it on a shelf, and say, "We're done. We built it. It's complete." You keep working on it, making it better and better for as long as you can (as good as you can). It's all aspirational, so identify what you want to become and work tirelessly toward that goal.

- There's no shortcut to creating an honest, values-driven organization. It takes commitment and a lot of hard work.

- Start out from day one building your brand the right way, defining and then embodying your values, so you don't lay down an unstable foundation.

CHAPTER TWO

Don't Focus on Winning

The whole notion behind winning is that if *you* win, someone else loses. There's always the victorious one and the defeated one, right? Isn't that how it's supposed to be in the business world? For my business to grow and thrive, someone else's business must die a hard death?

Here's another popular notion. As entrepreneurs, we're supposed to strive for hockey stick growth, because that's what *real* winning looks like. First, you grow steadily for a while. Then, by some dramatic and strategic turn of events, you suddenly rocket toward insane growth and crush the competition so badly that their children's children will feel the pain.

That's the way it's *supposed* to go, or so the business culture would have us believe. Here, let's reduce it to a simple, shitty equation:

Hockey stick growth + annihilating the competition = true business success.

But what if our business culture was a bit more like an old-growth forest. You've got the towering titan of the forest rising up a hundred feet or more, a massive tree that has grown slowly and consistently over many years. Around it, much younger and smaller trees have sprouted up, ten or fifteen feet tall but growing patiently. Eventually, the titan collapses, either from age, internal rot, or some change in the environment, and when it does, it opens a massive gap in the canopy overhead—a perfect opportunity for one of those steadily growing smaller trees to stretch out and take its place.

But all of the trees, no matter their size, are growing methodically, taking their time to do it right, growing patiently to capitalize on an opportunity when it happens. They're growing sustainably, which ensures that they can stay in the game a very long time, and the symbiotic and communal environment of the old-growth forest provides additional stability.

That's not how most business leaders want to grow because we are trained to think growth and only growth, no matter what. So we seek hacks to catapult our brands into the stratosphere overnight. It's like a lonely tree sprouting up suddenly in the middle of a gravel parking lot. It lacks support, it lacks community, it hasn't grown in a normal, healthy way, and the roots are probably shallow. That poor freak of a tree isn't going to last long. The first strong wind is going to knock it over. And that'll be the end of it.

The average lifespan of a company in the early half of the twentieth century was sixty-seven years. These days, the average lifespan of a small business is about eight-and-a-half years.[3] That's a drastic reduction in business life expectancy. What accounts for this dramatic change? In my experience, just like our gravel parking lot tree, it is mostly the result of bad growth.

Let's face it, we've lost our way. Far too many business leaders bow down to the pressure of being successful as fast as possible. They're only focused on winning quickly, not staying in the game as long as possible. They don't think much about their growth's impact on the rest of the world, and their egos are out of control. They want their companies to become the titan tree overnight, and they'll burn the whole forest down around them, if they have to, in order to achieve it. They want all of the credit, all of the money, and none of the blame.

That is not healthy, and it's not sustainable. With that approach, the long-term health of the business doesn't really matter, just the overnight success story that might be coming to a business website near you.

3   https://www.nav.com/small-business-statistics/

But what's the collateral damage of these kinds of business decisions to the people in those companies, to their industry, to the world, or to the reputations of those leaders and their brands?

Ultimately, there's not a lot that's in our control, but what we *can* control are the actions we take, the decisions we make, and the words we say. We can choose to play the small-business game in a way that we'll be proud of. We can choose to grow the right way, with engaged and fulfilled employees, meaningful relationships with customers, and a stellar reputation that we've earned from being decent human beings. We can choose to do that, no matter what the world, our industry, or our business environment is like.

Profit Center or Expense?

Years ago, I was hired by a large beer wholesaler in Philadelphia to work in their sign shop. My team and I worked on designing posters, ads, and banners—a lot of hands-on design work. This was only my second job in the industry, but I wound up becoming a leader in the business. I created a department from the ground up, put together a stellar team, created an internship program, and busted my ass to improve all of our processes and build a high-performing department.

There was just one problem: they wouldn't pay me a decent salary. In my previous job, I'd made the equivalent of $20 an hour (in the year 2000, that wasn't too shabby), but this company refused to pay me more than $12. Despite the fact that I had two college degrees, hired and managed staff for the department, and was directly responsible for supporting a marketing-leading sales team,, I found myself working three jobs just to make ends meet. Anytime I asked the director for a raise, I was told, "There's just no more money in the budget."

I wasn't stupid. I knew how it worked. The money was there. The company was doing very well. He just didn't want to pay me more, because he wanted to keep more for himself. When the owner of the company looked at my department, he saw the couple hundred-thousand dollars being spent on salaries and supplies as a burden to be minimized by any means possible. He didn't weigh the cost against how we were impacting sales growth. In reality we were a profit center, not an expense, but he wanted to pay me and the rest of my team as little as he could get away with. While he thought he was saving money for the company's priorities, the low pay for the design team eventually came at a much larger price.

My story is hardly unique. In fact, with record numbers of people leaving their jobs (what experts are calling the Great Resignation), our society has reached a tipping point because many talented, hard-working people feel *exactly* the same way: underpaid, underappreciated, and overworked by business owners who selfishly want to hoard power and money, no matter what damage they inflict on their employees, teams, and society.

But what's the real cost for treating your people like shit? If you care anything about your reputation, the cost is immense. For one, you'll create a culture of apathy. Do you really want to pay anyone any amount to work for you when they just don't give a fuck? You may also be creating a culture of contempt, where they *do* give a fuck, but not about doing great work for your company. Instead, they look for ways to pay you back for how miserable you make them feel.

Treat people like dirt, and they'll do the same to your brand and your company forever.

The Jig Is Up

Ten years after that job with the beer wholesaler, I'd moved from in-house work to become the senior leader at an agency. However, the agency had it's only problem: their only tangible metric for "success" was selling. In leadership meetings, it was the one and only thing that was talked about, celebrated, and (aside from billable hours) measured.

As you can imagine, this led to a culture of apathy and shitty delivery (if anything was delivered at all). Many projects were never completed, and if they were, they were only "good enough" at best. There were projects I worked on for as long as eighteen months that still weren't close to completion when I moved on.

Brands that focus too heavily on transactions are losing customers and talent at an increasingly faster rate. No longer can a brand promise the world just to get a client's money and then deliver a half-assed result. This will never be a sustainable business model. The younger generations, in particular, see right through it, and for brands that do it, things are only going to get worse. The jig is up. Increasingly, people are unwilling to work for or tolerate brands that operate this way.

So what should we do? It's very clear: Become purpose driven. While this can mean becoming a B Corp or operating like Patagonia, it can also simply mean you have a purpose greater than profit. Rather than just trying to make as much money as possible by any means at your disposal, you're trying to make life better in some way for your customers, for your team members, for your community, and for the world.

More than ever, people insist on connecting with relatable companies who share their values and actually give a damn about something other than making the owner and shareholders rich. When you really think about how most companies are run, it's kind of sickening. Behind it all, the singular motive driving absolutely everything is to make as much money as possible for a tiny, select group of people at the expense of everyone else.

Do you honestly believe a company like Amazon gives a shit about anyone or anything other than making Jeff Bezos and a select few leaders and shareholders filthy rich? The same could be said of Facebook. How much dangerous misinformation has been spread by that social media platform, misinformation that threatens the fabric of civilization and democracy.

But who cares about civilization and democracy, right? The real goal is to make Zuckerberg a billionaire so he can buy up hundreds of acres of pristine Hawaiian land while he rides his stupid fucking hydrofoil.

We have companies literally destroying the planet to line the pockets of a relatively small number of people, decimating the environment, creating slave-like working conditions, and they still have the audacity to try to paper over their wretchedness with gimmicks, cheap slogans, and phony "values." It's no different than an authoritarian country run by a brutal dictator. All the government propaganda in the world doesn't hide the fact that the whole system exists to acquire, maintain, and protect the wealth and power of the maniac in the stupid uniform sitting on the ridiculous-looking throne.

It doesn't have to be this way. There are some companies proving this every day. Companies that make it clear they appreciate their employees and try to make real connections with their target audience. If this book achieves nothing else, I hope it at least provokes you to spend some time being introspective about the business decisions you're making.

If you're solely focused on winning, on growing as fast as possible by any means possible in order to line your own pockets, then you're playing a short-sighted game. It's all going to catch up to you eventually. People will see through it. They'll see who you really are, not who you pretend to be.

But ultimately, you get to choose who you're going to be. With every decision you make, you either help or hurt the reputation of your brand and of yourself. I mean, for fuck's sake, do you really want people to look at you the way the general public looks at Zuckerberg or Bezos? Yes, you might become a billionaire, but you'll also be a laughingstock to most of the world, and they'll piss on your fucking grave when you're gone.

What if you stopped looking solely at winning— what if you just retired that word from your dictionary—and focused on success instead? I mean, what is success anyway?

In my opinion, success is growing a business through an authentic focus on real values, creating real connections with your customers, and consistently delivering value while making your employees feel like they are more than just cogs in a machine. It's building a proven reputation as a business leader who clearly gives a shit about something other than filling up his own bank vault so he can swim in the gold coins while the whole world laughs at him.

Chapter Two Reflections:

► We can choose to grow the right way, with engaged and fulfilled employees, meaningful relationships with customers, and a stellar reputation that we've earned from being decent human beings.

► What's the real cost for treating your people like shit? In doing so, you create a culture of apathy and contempt.

► Rather than just trying to make as much money as possible, reduce expenses and raise profits, you can commit to making life better in some way for your customers, your team members, your community, and the world.

► Success is growing a business through an authentic focus on real values, creating real connections with your customers, and consistently delivering value while making your employees feel like they are more than just cogs in a machine.

CHAPTER THREE

Build Your Reputation

Many companies operate with such razor-thin profit margins that they are basically unviable. Somehow, they need to make millions of dollars a year on the backs of minimum-wage workers just so a select few leaders can live well.

When you think about it, that's an absurd business model. A business like that doesn't deserve to exist. The City of Baltimore implemented a two-cent soda tax in 2010, and a lot of businesses complained.

I remember the owner of one particular corner store making a big stink about it. "We've been in this same location for forty years," he said, "and now we're going to have to close shop because of this soda tax. If this goes through, we'll leave the city!"

And my reaction at the time was, "Your entire business is selling sugar water. If adding a two-cent tax is more than you can handle, then your business probably shouldn't exist anyway. That's your fault. You created an unviable business model with a razor-thin profit margin selling sugar water to kids and poor people."

Nowadays, I would broaden that response and say, "If a company can't compete in the modern market, pay taxes, and contribute to the very society that their employees and customers exist in, then they probably shouldn't exist."

Do the Right Thing

One of the catalysts for starting my own company was my growing contempt for the whole marketing and advertising world. So much of it is focused solely on transactions. Plenty of companies will sell people exactly what they want, but that doesn't mean they can (or will, or intend to) deliver it. Often, they sell it just to close a deal, then cross their fingers and hope they can figure out how to deliver the thing they've sold.

If, instead, they vetted clients based on what they can actually provide, then they would be destined for success. Every business transaction would be a self-fulfilling prophecy, guaranteed to make the client happy. From that would flow referrals, positive reviews, and recommendations. There would be greater employee engagement as well because teams want to work with happier and more profitable clients.

Instead of catering to the owner's greed, closing every transaction you can in order to line their pockets, you'd build a brand based on a clear understanding of who you are, what you stand for, and what you can deliver. That was my purpose in starting my own agency. At Propr, we know who we are and what we stand for. We know the reputation we want to build, and every decision we make, every action we take, is aspirational.

I know if we take on the wrong project just so we can close another deal, we'll only be hurting ourselves one way or another. Just because we *can* do something doesn't mean we *should* do something.

Growing up, we're often told, "Do what makes you happy in life." The implication is that your own personal happiness is the most important thing in the world, but it seems like a terrible message to me. It creates a culture of self-centeredness, where everyone is doing whatever is best for them without regard to the broader implications of their actions.

The irony is that a lot of people who are singularly focused on their own personal happiness wind up being really fucking miserable, so they put on a façade of happiness. Another form of "fake it until you make it." Self-serving, ego-stroking people trying to feel important and cool, trying to be big shots—and few of them are actually happy. Meanwhile, everyone thinks they're kind of pathetic and mocks them from a distance.

What the hell is the point? Like I said, do you really want to be the weird rich guy riding the hydrofoil and holding the American flag as you decimate civilization and the whole world makes fun of you? Is that really happiness?

Personally, I'm determined *not* to be that guy, and I don't want my agency modeled after that kind of thinking. When we got fired by the espresso company for offending the owner's wife over her web design, I knew there were changes I had to make to prevent such a thing from ever happening again. But the truth is, the company never should have taken on the project in the first place. It was a bad fit, and if the sales team had been more values-driven, rather than just trying to close any deal they could, they would have realized it was a bad fit. For one thing, they would have discovered that the wife of the owner had designed the existing website and felt protective of it.

We never obtained that information until it was too late because the company got excited about the money. They wanted to close any transaction they could to bring in more money. After we got fired from that project, the owner of the agency summoned me and the other project manager into the conference room, and he proceeded to yell at us until he was red in the face. He expected us to take full blame for the project's failure, but I refused to be bullied or intimidated by the guy.

"We did everything right, but we were set up for failure," I replied. "We were never told that the client's wife was part of the company, let alone a key decision-maker and the designer of the website. We couldn't possibly have predicted that our redesign would be too painful for her because we didn't even know she was involved."

Bear in mind, the owner of the agency was the walking stereotype of everything I've decried in this book. He wore only tailored shirts and drove a giant, fancy SUV. He thought he was a big shot, and in his own mind, he was part of high society. His whole persona was Mr. Big Deal, and he constantly fed his own ego.

On one occasion, a friend of mine who owned a fashion boutique invited me to be in their annual fashion show as a runway model. It was a hilarious idea, so I did it. We got drunk and had a blast, and I walked the catwalk.

However, Mr. Big Deal saw pictures of the event on social media, and he approached me and said, "How the hell did you end up as a fashion model?"

"Oh, I know the boutique owner," I replied. "She asked me to participate. It was a lot of fun."

I could tell by the expression on the boss's face that he was hurt and jealous. And then he had the audacity to claim, "Well, you know, they asked me to do it, too, but I couldn't."

I later talked to my friend and said, "Oh, you asked Mr. Big Deal to do the catwalk, too?"

And my friend replied, "What? No. I don't even know who that is."

The owner only got more and more insecure and insufferable over time, even as he strove to keep up the "Mr. Big Deal in Tailored Shirts" persona. All I could do was try my best to be a decent person, even as I continued to work for him. I tried to really connect with the staff, customers, and community. Over time, customers began to assume I was the owner of the agency because of the relationships I developed with them. That made the boss even more hostile and insecure. Finally, I just had to leave the company.

Good *and* Successful

Greed and selfishness. They're everywhere. Even now, when people ask me about my company, they usually ask questions like, "How many employees do you have?" As if that metric matters. Or, "Have you worked with any well-known clients?" That doesn't matter either.

The only questions that really matter are, "How am I treating other people? How do they feel working at this agency? How am I improving the lives of our clients and customers? How is our business getting better?"

I don't ever want to be one of those companies that brags about making $10 million while their overhead is $9.97 million. Of course, I'm not running a charity. We have to be profitable, but I'm determined to be both good *and* financially successful. I refuse to pillage, burn, and salt the earth just so I can put up a front like Mr. Big Deal.

Dan Price, the CEO of the credit card processing company Gravity Payments, became famous in recent years because he started paying all of his employees a $75,000 salary. He also stopped paying himself 300 percent more than everyone else. I like that. I like it a lot.

At the same time, it's sad that we've gone so far in the other direction that Dan's decision is shocking. Paying every employee a decent salary and not keeping all of the money for yourself shouldn't even be newsworthy. *Of course* you should pay your people well, for fuck's sake. *Of course* you should pay your interns. They're contributing to your success, so treat them fairly.

To be brutally honest, all of the continued publicity and self-promotion about Dan's salary scheme seems a bit fishy to me. If you're doing the right thing just to boast about doing the right thing, then maybe you're not actually doing the right thing.

As Tywin Lannister said in *Game of Thrones* to his insufferable, evil grandson King Joffrey, "Any man who must say, 'I am the king,' is no true king." A good leader doesn't have to tell you constantly that they are good, just like the smartest kid in school doesn't have to tell you they are smart, and the toughest kid on the playground doesn't have to tell people they are the toughest.

If you have to keep positioning yourself as a moral authority, then you might not be a moral authority anymore. At that point, it's posturing. What if it's possible to run a successful business while treating people well because you value treating people well?

The world would definitely be a better place and people would want to work for (and with) your company.

Chapter Three Reflections:

▸ If a company can't compete in the modern market, pay taxes, and contribute to the very society that their employees and customers exist in, they probably shouldn't exist.

▸ Instead of catering to the owner's greed, closing every transaction you can in order to line the pockets of a tiny group of people, build a brand based on a clear understanding of who you are, what you stand for, and what you can deliver.

▸ Of course you should pay your people fairly, for fuck's sake.

▸ What if it's possible to run a successful business while treating people well because you value treating people well?

CHAPTER FOUR

Authentic Leadership

A piece of advice. If anyone in your company is a micromanager, fire them immediately. Don't finish reading this sentence or sleep on it, do it as soon as you finish reading this sentence. Why? Because anybody who has the time and desire to micromanage other people clearly doesn't have a job. Why keep them around? Are you really going to continue paying someone a six-figure salary just so they can boss everyone around?

Do you remember that scene from the movie *Office Space* where the engineer liaison is asked by the two Bobs, "What would you say you do here?" And he can't give a reasonable answer, so he finally screams, "I have people skills! I am good at dealing with people! Can't you understand that? What the hell is wrong with you people?" He's promptly fired.

If you have any intention at all of creating a healthy company culture, the micromanagers and, in many cases, middle managers have to go. They're proving to you that they're unqualified to do their own jobs, since they apparently have plenty of time and energy to pester other people. Get rid of them promptly and replace them with people you can trust.

In fact, if you're under the delusion that you *need* micromanagers, it's probably because you've hired a bunch of people you *don't* trust. "Someone's got to keep an eye on my team at all times," you think, so you let the toxic culture continue.

Be Trustworthy and Direct

By the way, if you really want to create a culture of trust, it starts with you. To trust others, you must first be trustworthy. Do what you say, and say what you mean. Always follow through on promises, and act with genuine integrity and sincerity. Think about it, how can employees or customers ever develop any kind of relationship with your brand if you're not trustworthy?

When I started looking at jobs after grad school, I was rather picky about the companies I applied to. I spent a little over a year doing freelance work. When I finally got an interview with an established agency I wanted to work for, I was ready to leave freelancing behind. I yearned to do reputable work for a well-known agency. In quick order, I applied, got an interview, and was in the mix for the job.

The interview went really well, and I left the company that day feeling optimistic. They promised to get back to me soon, but weeks passed without any decision. I continued to follow up, and finally demanded to know either way, but I only got more of the same: "Don't worry. We really like you. Sit tight, and you'll hear from us soon."

Finally, ten weeks passed. It was Christmas Eve, and I still hadn't heard anything from them. I was depressed and frustrated by their lack of communication and compassion. I let my freelance work slide, which left me with little to do and a gaping unknown in my future. At the time, my wife and I were engaged, and we headed out to do some holiday shopping to try and lift my spirits. While I was incredibly frustrated with the company at this point, I tried not to think about it.

Five o'clock had rolled around, and we were motoring across town, when the president of the company finally called me.

"Hey there," he said, "we've decided to offer you the job. Do you want it?"

I was already in a foul mood, so I promptly declined the offer. It never should have taken so long to get back to me. In fact, if you're confident in your leadership and brand, you should be able to make a hiring decision almost on the spot.

A few years ago, I brought a guy on board to do some contract work for us with copywriting and account management. He was an older guy with a great resume, and he'd been director of digital marketing at a local university. I planned to connect him with a new client who was an important referral from one of our largest clients at the time. However, when he first showed up at the office to run the kickoff meeting with the client, he naively asked, "Where's my desk and computer?"

"Uh, dude, you're a contractor," I replied. "You don't have a desk or computer. Of course, if you want to work here in our office, you're more than welcome. We've got the space."

"But I need a computer," he replied. "I don't have one."

"You're a freelance digital marketer and a writer," I said. "Go down to the Apple store and get a MacBook Air for $1,200. They'll give you credit."

Something about this exchange just didn't add up. How could an independent contractor, freelance writer, digital marketer, and industry vet not have his own computer? Why would he expect a company that he was contracting with for a temporary gig to provide him with one? It was strange, but rather than waste the man's time, string him along, or drag it out, I let him go right away. While it forced me to reschedule the kickoff on the project, I was honest with the client and they understood. Then I immediately called the guy and let him know.

"I wish you the best, but I don't think this is going to work out," I said.

He wasn't happy about it, to say the least, but the point is, as soon as I saw I'd made the wrong choice, I took action, fixed it, and learned from it. I didn't drag it out, and I was honest with the client. I didn't worry about the perception of making a hard decision or having to reschedule. I was only concerned about being honest and forthcoming with these people (both the client and the contractor).

But that's not how it usually works with hiring practices. Instead, a company will bring in six different people and conduct six hours of interviews because they have no idea *who* they're hiring or *what* they're hiring for, and no one wants to be responsible if the decision turns out to be wrong. So they'll string candidates along for ages as they struggle to step up and make a decision.

If this is the case with your organization, empower your leaders to own their decisions and act fast (this goes both ways; take fast strategic action on both sides, whether you're correct or incorrect), and as long as they do their due diligence, there is no wrong decision, only learning opportunities.

Why We Hire Micromanagers

So, how do companies end up with micromanagers? It's simple, really. Leaders hire micromanagers to insulate themselves from their own people, who they do not like or trust.

Years ago, while working at an agency in Delaware, I started getting courted by a recruiter in Maryland. For a while, I resisted the offer, but when a relationship with a girlfriend ended, I decided to go for it. Suddenly, the idea of moving to a new city and getting a fresh start sounded awesome and since I no longer had anything holding me back, I went for it.

In the end, I interviewed with five different people at the company, which meant five separate trips to Maryland, before they offered me the job. In hindsight, it was a huge red flag and should have been a warning sign. But I was young and eager, so I accepted the offer.

As it turned out, my supervisor at the new company was a quintessential "middle management" yesman. On the one hand, he would try to encourage me by saying, "We hired you for your mind," but on the other hand, he punished me for having too many ideas and not sitting at my desk and doing exactly as

I was told by the brand managers. A very strong "sit down and shut up" vibe developed. As an idea guy, this was incredibly oppressive and painful for me.

Here's the thing, as MCA of the Beastie Boys said, "I'm an idea man, not a yes-man." I tried bringing in fresh ideas and pushing people a little bit out of their comfort zones, which is exactly what they'd hired me to do, but the more I tried to contribute, the more their contempt for me grew. It got to the point where my supervisor couldn't walk past me without scowling.

Bear in mind, I just wanted to improve processes and challenge some company dogma that was holding us back. I wasn't attacking anyone or insulting anything—I was trying to contribute in a meaningful, creative way. Company leaders knew that's the kind of guy I am before they hired me. Hell, it's the *reason* they hired me, or so they said. But in practice, they hated their dogma, processes, or status quo being challenged, and the boss made this very clear by how he treated me. Honestly, looking back, they never should have hired me. I was the wrong person for that place.

At the same time, my boss was clearly just a "yes man" to the company owners, and at the same time, like everyone else in the company, he was always trying to cover his own ass. That meant a steady stream of interruptions and distractions as he constantly intruded on what everyone was doing, and encouraged the brand managers to do the same. The boss absolutely loved any excuse to scold people, which created an incredibly toxic environment.

On one occasion, I had to leave work fifteen minutes early to catch a carpool. No big deal, right? We came in early and stayed late all the time, so it all came out in the wash sooner or later. However, as I walked into the building the next morning, the boss called me into his office to ask me, "When did I approve that time off?"

How does someone even respond to a question like that? It was fifteen minutes.

So I was getting two conflicting messages all the time. "We hired you for your mind," and "Sit down, shut up, and do what you're told?" It was, hands down, the worst job and worst experience I've ever had. The owners allowed and enabled this middle-management asshole to create an insufferable work environment for everyone, and he got off on it. He enjoyed making life miserable for me, and he made no effort to hide his contempt for me.

Chances are, you've worked for a boss like that. Haven't we all? Micromanaging jerk bosses are a dime a dozen, sadly, and company owners don't seem to mind. When I became an entrepreneur and started my own agency, I was determined to create a culture of trust, where I could trust my people, earn their trust, and *let go*. That means letting go of running the day-to-day, letting go of art direction, trusting my people to handle things, and accepting that if they screw up or make a mistake, it's not the end of the world.

I'll be the first to say, this isn't easy. In fact, it might be just about the hardest thing in the world for an entrepreneur. But what's the alternative? Micro-managing your team, constantly being in the way of people getting shit done, and making everyone terrified of making a mistake or losing a client? Fuck that. Honestly, when you're focused on building a brand you truly care about, letting go and empowering your people is the only way you'll ever succeed.

You've heard this from company leaders before, I'll bet: "We love our employees. We're a family here." Yeah, they all say it, but don't you dare rock the boat, leave work fifteen minutes early, or challenge company dogma, or you *will* get sucker-punched first thing the next morning.

Dare to Trust People

It's crazy to me that companies will pay people a bunch of money to micromanage and make their work environment miserable. What a waste of money. Here's a wild idea. What if you didn't hire *any* micromanagers? What if, instead, you hired trustworthy people and then treated them like adults, with respect? What if you were brave enough to give those trustworthy people a bit of autonomy?

Do you realize how much money you would save? More importantly, do you realize how much healthier, happier, and more productive your work culture would be? If you've never thought about this before, I hope it'll be a wakeup call for you.

At another workplace, I had a supervisor who was constantly on everyone's ass about everything. He was the middle manager between me (the art director) and the director of marketing. He gave us autonomy, but he liked to come in periodically and threaten or scold us. On one occasion, someone bitched at him about something, so he stormed into the production room and started threatening us.

"I'll move my desk in here," he shouted. "I'll move it right into the corner of the room!"

"Go ahead," I said, calling his bluff.

He backed off, but I went to the director of marketing and said, "Why is this guy between us? Why did you add this entirely unnecessary level of management to the company? It only introduces extra complexity to everyday tasks."

"It's because I didn't want to be bothered by the previous people who ran your department," he confessed, "but it's different now. Let's get rid of the middle management."

Bear in mind, middle managing my team wasn't even the guy's job. He'd been roped into the task. There was no good reason for it.

The recurring gag about Milton's red stapler in *Office Space* rings true. Micromanagers are constantly making arbitrary decisions and messing with people simply to flex their authority. You've experienced this somewhere. We all have. The business world is infested with pointless micromanagers who are constantly messing with employees for no good reason.

In my experience, you get the best out of your people when you engage them in a way that shows you trust them. Treat them with respect and let them do what you hired them to do. Why the hell wouldn't you want to do that? The only possible reason is because you're insecure, selfish, or intentionally trying to keep talented people in your company from shining too brightly and overshadowing your mediocrity.

If you want to create a culture of excellence, micromanaging must be excised completely like a cancerous tumor. Get it out of your culture completely. Don't overburden your people with unnecessary levels of management and bureaucracy. Save the money you'd spend on that useless mid-management jerk and use it to provide the help and resources your employees need to be successful. Then trust them and let them do the work you hired them to do! That's authentic leadership.

Oh, and while you're at it, you might as well purge all of your company's dogma, because it's also getting in the way.

—

Chapter Four Reflections:

▸ If anyone in your company is a micromanager, fire them immediately.

▸ If you want to create a culture of excellence, micromanaging must be excised completely like a cancerous tumor.

▸ Owners and senior leaders, this is on you. Don't allow and enable middle management assholes to create an insufferable work environment for everyone.

▸ Create a culture of trust. Be trustworthy yourself, hire trustworthy people, and treat them like adults.

▸ If you are confident in your leadership and brand, you should be able to make a hiring decision almost on the spot. Don't lead people on or waste their time.

PART TWO

Building Your Brand the Right Way

CHAPTER FIVE

No Dogma

Question everything. It's the only way toward growth and improvement.

There, that was simple enough. Chapter complete!

Of course, we need processes in order to reproduce success, and every process needs a starting point, but if you don't question everything and seek constant improvement, then you won't learn from your failures or improve.

Do you remember how your algebra teacher always made you show your work on tests? If you're like me, it always kind of annoyed you. "If I get the right answer, then who cares how I got it?" But, of course, your teacher wasn't just interested in the answer; they also wanted to make sure you used the best process for getting there (and didn't cheat).

When I hire a designer, I always ask them about their creative process. I want to hear about it, and I want to see it. It's important to have insight into the way they think and approach creativity because without a clear process, success is just luck, and no one builds a reputation through luck. But even a good process has to be questioned regularly. As computer pioneer Grace Murray Hopper famously said, "The most dangerous phrase in the English language is, 'We have always done it this way.'"

Even so, when I ask people the question, "Why do you do it this way?" I hear the same response all too often: "Well, that's just the way we've always done it."

Any process, no matter how well-designed and goal-oriented, becomes "just the way we've always done it" after a couple of revolutions around the sun. Suddenly, aspects of the process that were intentionally designed to meet very specific goals are now being replicated without much thought. Maybe they don't even serve their original purpose anymore, and already people have forgotten why they do it that way. The people who designed the initial process might be long gone. This is the birth of dogma.

Seriously, folks, don't be afraid to reevaluate everything—and I mean *everything*—regularly. For example, if you've created some five-step process that your company follows, you should periodically revisit all five of those steps and see if they can be improved or adjusted to meet your current needs better. You don't have to reinvent the wheel every time. It's perfectly fine to keep the processes and procedures that still work.

I'm being honest, standard operating procedures (SOPs) make me nervous. I don't like them. I know we have to set standards, but it's really easy for standardized processes to stagnate, or worse, become unquestionable dogma.

It doesn't take long for an ingrained process to become gospel that is too sacred to question. The people who designed the process and created the SOP eventually pass it on to new people, and since those new people weren't there to design it and might not fully understand the reasoning behind its design, they tend to simply accept it as an infallible dogma of the company.

Question Your Gospel

I know a guy who worked for an events-planning company doing sketches and stage designs for big events. When he got hired, he was incredibly excited and hyped, raring to go, but he didn't last more than a few months. I ran into him one day not long after, and he looked rather dejected. When I asked him what was wrong, he told me he'd been laid off.

"They said I was stuck in my ways," he explained. "They told me I just did things the way I'd always done them, and I wouldn't learn anything new. According to my boss, I was sabotaging the company."

I expressed sympathy, but then he said, "Hey, man, I heard you started your own agency. Could we grab a beer sometime and shoot the shit? I'd like to hear about it."

I had a long day ahead of me, but I said, "Yeah, sure, let's get together this evening."

I had to visit three different clients that day, and they were located all over Baltimore, so I spent hours cruising around the harbor on my little Honda Ruckus scooter. Afterward, I drove all the way back to a local bar in my neighborhood in order to meet with the guy. As we sat there chatting, he kept asking me about my company. It soon became clear that he wanted me to offer him a job.

Finally, I asked him, "What do you really love to do? And what are you really good at?"

And he replied, "Oh, man, I'm really into branding."

"What do you mean by branding?" I asked.

"You know, designing logos and stuff," he said.

"There's a hell of a lot more to branding before you get to designing logos," I said. "What about positioning? What about defining the reputation you want to create?"

"Yeah, I get all that," he said, "but I'd really like to design logos for your agency. I'd work part time.

That's gotta be worth about $10,000 a year. What do you say?"

"Well, what have you done? Show me some samples of your work."

He opened the photos on his phone and showed me the logo he'd created for a local coffee shop. "This company is now worth $1.2 million," he boasted, "and I designed the logo for them."

"When did you create their logo?" I asked.

"About sixteen years ago," he replied, "but they're a successful company now. My design must have played a big role in their growth. It's what I do. I design logos! It's what I've always done!"

"You designed a logo based on what the owner wanted," I reminded him, "and then he built the company, and you're taking credit for his success?"

At this point, I could tell he was getting offended, so I tried to clarify my point.

"These days, hiring someone to design a logo is worth about $200," I said, "but you want me to hire you part-time to design logos for $10,000. Unless you have a process and a history of results that can clearly tie your logo design to the success of your client companies, then you're asking for way more than you're worth. The fact that you designed a logo for a successful company sixteen years ago doesn't demonstrate that you bring much value, so why would I hire you? You need to rethink your business model and what you're actually offering."

It was the final straw. Convinced I was insulting him, he stood up, red-faced, and said, "Hey, man, do we need to step outside?"

"Sit down," I replied. "How dare you! I've driven all over town today working with clients, and rather than going home to my family, I came here to meet with you and give you some advice. I'm not trying to insult your skills. I'm trying to help you understand how you can build a business! In the past, you made a living designing logos, but it's not enough anymore. You have to change your approach if you want clients and companies to see the value in hiring you for your asking price."

Unfortunately, at this point, he started crying and lamenting his life, the recent breakup of his marriage, and other woes, and the conversation took a rather pitiful turn. I felt bad for the guy, but at the same time, it was baffling that he took my advice as an insult. I was trying to get him to reevaluate his approach so he could achieve his career goals, but he reacted like I'd stabbed his sacred cow.

And where does that guy work today? At the coffee shop. He's a barista. It's a noble enough profession, but he's definitely not designing logos for a living.

At one time in his life, designing logos might have been enough to make a decent living, but times have changed. He needed to change with them. He needed to offer a lot more, but he just wouldn't let go of "the way I've always done it." And it brought his design career to an end.

It's such a common problem that I could fill a book just with examples of this one thing.

1. A process or approach is designed in a specific way because it works or meets a need.

2. That process or approach becomes gospel.

3. Nobody in the company wants to question the gospel.

When I worked for the company with the micro-managing asshole boss, they had a certain process in place once our designs were printed. First, they went to legal to make sure everything was kosher. Then they went to *all* of the managers of the company, which meant about twenty different leaders looked at the designs, and each of them would take a Sharpie or a highlighter and mark up the designs with their feedback.

When you finally got the printouts of your designs back, they were covered in so many scribbles, you could barely read what anyone had written. It was absolutely ridiculous and in no way helpful to the design team.

Finally, I approached the leadership and said, "Why are leaders who have nothing to do with our department scribbling all over our designs? Why the hell is the director of customer service giving us design feedback? And for that matter, why do we have to print them out when we could just send them as PDFs so we can track edits and revisions? Then the leaders could write their notes and attach them to the file without making a big mess. As it is, we're sending these printed packets around, and they're three inches thick, held together by alligator clips, and you guys are writing all over each other and covering each other's notes. It's incredibly inefficient, and we're losing time and making errors as a result."

To drive home the point, I added, "You've given carte blanche to every manager in the company to direct your design team, and we can't even track all of the comments or figure out who they came from. Then you get mad at us because we can't interpret some random manager's highlighter marks buried among a hundred other comments. We've been set up for failure. With PDFs, we would know who individual comments came from, so we would know who to talk to if we had any questions."

How did the leaders respond to my suggestions? Did they say, "Wow, good job on your creative problem-solving for our broken system? You just saved us thousands of dollars a year on expensive printers, not to mention all the extra time we will have! And our designers will be so much less frustrated!"

No, of course not. The system was their gospel, and it was not to be tampered with. They were furious, and my micromanaging boss resented me more than ever.

But why? Why do some leaders get so angry when you suggest changing or improving the way they do things? I think the answer is simple: control. That's what it comes down to. Having dogmas that can't be questioned gives company leaders a measure of control, and it also allows them to cover their own asses.

"Don't you dare question our busted system! Don't you dare expose our inefficiencies! This is holy ground upon which you walk!"

Ultimately, as I said, it's important to have processes in place. Being able to show your team and your clients *how* you are going to achieve success is absolutely vital for communicating the value of what you do. However, I will continue to state emphatically that I do not believe your processes should become gospel. Always keep them open to evaluation, criticism, questions, and improvements.

There are always going to be ways to get better, to remove complexity, inefficiencies, and unnecessary expenses. Have an open mind to change. Seek improvement with your brand always. Don't be afraid of change. Embrace it! It's the only way toward improvement and growth.

Chapter Five Reflections:

▶ Question everything. It's the only way toward improvement and growth.

▶ It's good to have processes, but any process, no matter how well-designed and goal-oriented, becomes "just the way we've always done it" after a couple of revolutions around the sun. Don't be afraid to reevaluate everything regularly.

▶ Your processes should never become gospel. There are always going to be ways to get better, to remove complexity, inefficiencies, and unnecessary expenses. Have an open mind to change!

▶ If you don't question everything and seek constant improvement, then you won't learn from your failures or improve.

CHAPTER SIX

It's Our Duty to Give Back

No one, and I mean absolutely no one, achieves success entirely on their own, simply through their own talent and hard work. There are always numerous contributing factors, and a lot of other people who help them along that path, providing the right information, opportunities, education, advice, coaching, money, and resources.

It's a bit like being the president. If anything goes wrong in the country, the president gets the full blame, because "the buck stops here," but in reality, numerous people contributed to the problem. Conversely, if the job market goes up, what does the media say? "The president added two million jobs this quarter!" While the president may have contributed significantly, a whole lot of other people were also directly responsible for the increase in jobs.

There are so many different people who contribute to the success of any individual. Yes, there are the macho types who like to pretend that they can do it all by themselves, but nobody ever really achieves success without the contributions of many others.

When the iPhone first hit the market in 2007, Steve Jobs didn't just create it by himself, and he wasn't inventing a whole new technology out of thin air. Rather, the iPhone was a product born out of almost two hundred years of technological innovation by thousands of men and women around the world, not to mention the hard work and innovation of all the Apple employees and their co-manufacturers.

One of the reasons I felt compelled to write this book in the first place is because of all the information I've gained from other people over the years. Through books, classes, music, and conversations, a whole hell of a lot of people have influenced me, informed me, and guided me to the point I'm at today. Yes, I worked very hard, but without the contributions of all of those other people, my hard work wouldn't have gotten me very far.

The same is true of you. Anything you've achieved in life has been at least partly the result of teachers, mentors, friends, coworkers, employees, writers, speakers, maybe parents, and others. We have to start giving credit and stop acting like we climbed our own mountain without any help. We need to be more honest and humble about our success.

Collective learning is an essential part of human development. In our early prehistory, humans gradu-ally developed the ability to speak and communicate, which enabled us to tell stories to each other. For bet-ter or worse, this put us on the trajectory that has led us to where we are today. Human civilization is, in a sense, a constant collective conversation, and that means we are continually learning from one another and being influenced by one another.

It's that collective conversation that put a man on the moon in 1969. That monumental achievement depended on countless generations of acquired knowledge, technological developments, pattern matching, and shared information.

Since every single goddamned one of us owes our success to the contributions of a lot of people who have given us the information, resources, and opportunities that we used to achieve success, the least we can do is give back. It's always a shame when some successful person acquires great experiences, incredible skills, and a vast amount of resources and then dies without passing them on. They spend their whole life taking from others—information, knowledge, training, mentoring, opportunities, money, time, whatever—create success for themselves with those things, and then run with them into a dead end. It's a waste and a disgrace.

Givers and Takers

You owe it to the world to give back a little bit for what you've been given. That means sharing your knowledge and wisdom. It means sharing the credit for your achievements. It might even mean giving some of your resources to create opportunities for others. We're all *takers*, but we have to choose whether or not we're going to be *givers* as well.

It's astonishing to me how little some companies want to give to the people who contribute to their success, people whose hard work lines the pockets of executives and shareholders. When a multi-million-dollar company operates under such slim margins that the only way they can survive is to pay their people as little as they can legally get away with, then maybe the world would be better off without them.

The wealthiest company in the world, Walmart, should not have employees making so little that they qualify for food stamps and Medicaid.[4] What the

4   https://www.cnbc.com/2020/11/19/walmart-and-mcdonalds-among-top-employers-of-medicaid-and-food-stamp-beneficiaries.html

fuck is wrong with the business world? Maybe you remember a few years ago when McDonald's created a financial planning guide for their low-wage workers that recommended working a second job for a sixty-hour work week and included a sample budget with absurdly low expenses, like $20 a month for healthcare, $600 rent, and a $150 car payment (but included no money for gas or food).[5]

When huge companies do shit like this, everyone hears the message loud and clear from the leaders to their workers: "Please work a sixty-hour week and apply for food stamps and Medicaid so we can continue to be multi-millionaires. Thanks!"

As a Gen Xer, I grew up in an era where many large corporations, faced with the prospect of having to pay people more, just fled the country and moved all of their factories to poverty-stricken third-world countries. And do we even need to get into how companies are devastating the environment and possibly

5   https://www.nbcnews.com/businessmain/
mcdonalds-finance-guide-insulting-low-wage-workers-6c10653604

destroying our future with global warming just to make a little more money?

The United States is the largest contributor to plastic waste in the world, with between 1.13 million to 2.24 million metric tons leaking into the environment each year. These plastics take hundreds of years to decompose, and the deluge of waste has been called "one of the biggest environmental threats facing our oceans and our planet today."

Fortunately, the EPA recently created a national recycling strategy that would help solve the problem, but some business leaders have complained. Why? Well, I'll let Joshua Baca, the vice president of plastics for The American Chemistry Council, share his "wisdom." In a statement, he said, "Unfortunately, the report also suggests restricting plastic production to reduce marine debris. This is misguided and would lead to supply chain disruptions."[6]

Pardon the sarcasm, but we simply *can't* be causing

6   https://www.washingtonpost.com/climate-environment/2021/12/01/plastic-waste-ocean-us/

supply chain disruptions just to do silly things like prevent a worldwide environmental catastrophe! That might trim some fat from the bloated profits of the select few, and that would be tragic.

Maybe you've seen the following comic from Tom Toro:

"Yes, the planet got destroyed. But for a beautiful moment in time we created a lot of value for shareholders."

Sarcasm aside, it doesn't do much good to point the finger at others if we're not also going to point the finger right back at ourselves. We have to ask ourselves if we're takers or givers. What would it mean for your company to become a giving company?

One thing no one ever told me was how amazing it feels as a business leader to change people's lives for the better. When you hire people, pay them a decent salary, and enable them to be active contributors to something meaningful—then support them in their work—it's just about the best feeling in the world.

And if an employee finds another opportunity and decides it's time to move on, there's no reason you can't continue to encourage them. As I always tell my people, "If this is no longer the right opportunity for you, then you owe us nothing. You've contributed, you got paid well for that contribution, and we appreciate what you've done. You don't have to hide your job hunt from us. We'll support you, even if that means making an introduction, giving a reference or a referral." And I've stuck to that fairly well, I think.

My company wouldn't exist without the contributions of my employees—neither would yours—so if they want to move on, they owe us nothing more. There's no reason to shit all over someone just because they want to go somewhere else. It's not a privilege for them to have a job with you, it is *your* privilege and honor that they work for you. There's no reason why you can't still encourage and support them all the way out the door and beyond. In fact, it is the least you can do.

I have a few employees at my agency who said prior to working here that they had vowed to never work for another creative agency. They'd had so many bad experiences with ego-driven micromanaging bosses and toxic cultures that they'd come to despise the whole agency world. Somehow, probably because I despise that stuff, too, I still managed to convince them to come work with me, and now they are thriving. They're happy, enthusiastic about coming to work, and feel fulfilled. And that's awesome.

What makes the difference? I like to think it's because I'm not trying to make as much profit as possible from them while giving them as little as I can get away with. I'm determined to create an environment of trust, autonomy, empowerment, and respect, where people are paid what they deserve to be paid, and respected for their talents, ability, and value they bring to the team. I want my employees to be successful, not just to line my own pockets but for their own happiness and fulfillment. And I have no reason *not* to do this, because they give the company so much.

A Time to Reflect

I encourage every business leader to spend some time reflecting on everyone who has contributed to their success. Consider the people who have given you the opportunities you took advantage of, the people who influenced you to make the right decisions, and the people who are contributing to your success right now.

And I'm not just talking about your financial success. Consider your health and happiness as well. Indeed, the people who only define success by money are the very ones who are a scourge to the earth. Making a lot of money but leaving burned-out employees and environmental ruin in your wake is not success. It is very clearly a failure.

In terms of your brand, you'd be a lot more successful, even if it meant making less money and not growing quite as big, if you focused on creating a good product with engaged employees while making a positive impact on the world to the best of your ability. We need a hell of a lot more business leaders who will chase that kind of success. Otherwise, we're all quite literally doomed.

If you're a taker, you might be protected from some of the worst consequences of your selfishness for the time being, but eventually they'll catch up with you. And if not you, then they'll catch up to your children and grandchildren, and that carnage you've left along your path will be your only legacy.

Sadly, a lot of business leaders would read this chapter and still not give a shit.

"Oh, well, I won't be here to worry about what my grandchildren have to deal with," they would think, even if they never say it out loud—even if they continued to verbally espouse values they don't care about or practice. That's some nihilist bullcrap if you ask me.

But maybe, just maybe, since you picked up this book, there's hope. Maybe you're someone who gives a shit and doesn't want the world to become a darker and darker place just to line your own pockets a little more—you just need some encouragement and a little nudge to make big changes.

The good news? You can still make a damn great amount of money, live in a really nice home, *and* give generously to your employees, customers, and the world. More than that, you can achieve success in business and leave a legacy behind that your friends, family, customers, and employees will be proud of. And I'm here to tell you that you have all of our permission to run your business the right way.

Chapter Six Reflections:

► It is an irrefutable fact: Many different people and factors contribute to the success of any individual.

► Since every single one of us owes our success to the contributions of a lot of people who have given us the information, resources, and opportunities that we used to achieve success, the least we can do is give back.

► When you hire people, pay them a decent salary, and enable them to be active contributors to something meaningful—then support them in their work. This is just about the best feeling in the world.

► My company wouldn't exist without the contributions of my employees—neither would yours—so if they want to move on, they owe us nothing more. There's no reason to shit all over someone just because they want to go somewhere else.

► You can make a damn good amount of money, live in a nice home, *and* give generously to your employees, customers, and the world. More than that, you can achieve success in business and leave a legacy behind that your friends, family, customers, and employees will be proud of.

CHAPTER SEVEN

Too Transactional

Does the success of your company require you to become a sociopath? It's a fair question when you consider the maniac billionaires who run some of the world's biggest companies. More to the point, what does success even look like? Judging by the behavior of some of the billionaires, success is only ever defined as acquiring absolutely as much money as you can without limit and by almost any means that you can get away with.

How much is enough, honestly? How much money does a single human being really need to hoard before we view it as a mental illness that cries out for treatment? You've probably seen, or at least heard of, the show *Hoarders*, in which these poor individuals have absolutely filled every square inch of their homes with junk and trash. In each episode, a team comes in to clean the house, throw all of the junk and trash away, and help the individual escape the trap of their own insatiable need to collect worthless stuff.

We look at these pitiful trash hoarders and feel sorry for them, but then we turn right around and look at hoarders like Jeff Bezos or Michael Bloomberg or Richard Branson, and say, "Wow, that guy should run for president. What a great leader!" Somehow, the hoarding of wealth is confused as a sign of wisdom and good leadership, rather than the mental and moral sickness that it is.

When someone is determined to hoard vastly more money than they could ever need or spend, with no limit to their appetite, is it really any different than some guy hoarding junk from floor to ceiling in his house? Is there anything normal or healthy about a guy who is driven by an insatiable greed that has no limit? Shouldn't we at least stop glorifying them?

Maybe we need a show like *Hoarders* for these guys, so we can start helping them overcome their unhealthy appetite for ridiculous amounts of money. It's not just the hoarding of power and wealth that is the issue; it's the cost the rest of society must pay through the exploitation of people, resources, the environment, and general well-being. While the person hoarding at home might impact a few people, the hoarding of power and wealth hurts the entire world.

A few months after I started my business, I was working in my home office one evening when my wife walked in with a little plastic stick in her hand and said, "According to this thing, I'm pregnant." We already had a two-year-old, and suddenly we were dealing with an unexpected pregnancy. Fast forward eight months, and my wife had gone back to work after our son was born.

She was given three months of leave, but once back, we quickly learned that the company wasn't accommodating to young mothers at all. Either they didn't realize that thirty-ish women still sometimes make babies, or they simply didn't care. Their attitude seemed to be, "We don't give a shit that you're a mother with a new baby. You work for us. Nothing should interfere with that ever." It's a completely irrational mindset, and it's grossly unfair to people. After putting up with it for almost two months, my wife said, "Fuck it," and quit.

By that point, Propr was about a year old, and now I was shouldering the financial burden for our family entirely on my own. I worked so hard during that period of time, and faced such a mountain of pressure, that I became physically sick. I had no time for my family, and the thought that kept running through my head was, "What's the point of having this business if I'm working myself to death and not enjoying life?"

I was literally living that old song *The Cat's in the Cradle*. "When you coming home, Dad? I don't know when. We'll get together then." And for what? Trying to rush success and losing my most precious and valuable resource along the way: *time*.

I talk with many entrepreneurs who share some version of the same story. It goes like this: "I got fed up with work, so I started my own company. Now, I work sixty hours a week for myself instead of working forty hours for someone else."

Fuck no. That's not a good thing. That's not why we start our own businesses! We do it to take control of our lives and careers. So I stopped playing that shitty sixty-hour-a-week game. These days, we focus on a healthy balance (of course, we have to put in the time now and again) and consistently delivering high value to our clients.

I refuse to chase money by overworking or robbing my family of time with me. I won't be the dad who comes home late from work, then keeps right on working in the home office all evening so his kids never see him. I recently saw a post on LinkedIn where a guy boasted about how he gets up before his family to start working, mingles with his family during the day while still putting time in, and gets back to work after the kids go to bed. That's not awesome or honorable—it's sad.

That's not success either. That's complete fucking failure, no matter how much money you acquire along the way. My son is currently in kindergarten, and if I have to leave work at 1:30 in the afternoon to pick him up from school, I'll do it, and then I'll pick up my daughter at 3:15. That's way more important to me than a few more hours of "grinding" or chasing money.

And I've given my team the exact same amount of flexibility and autonomy. That's success to me. Somehow, we're still able to build and grow our brand every year.

Hell, one of the reasons I started my own company in the first place was because of how disgusted I was at the way so many agencies are run. Leaders maximize revenue per employee and revenue per customer, and *that's it*. That is their whole strategy for creating success. Every single goddamned decision that's ever made is about trying to get more and more productivity out of employees, more and more dollars out of clients, to really bleed them dry in order to attract more customers in order to generate more revenue. And that's it. It's a very simple, soul-destroying machine. But it doesn't have to be that way. It's a choice.

They say they want to develop strong relationships with employees and customers, but in practice, the only thing that ever matters is money coming in. "Grab every transaction you can by any means you can get away with and hide behind brand values while you do it." That's why so many big companies have abandoned the US for the third world. That's why they outsource as much as they can outsource. They're not trying to provide jobs for people in India or the Philippines. They don't give a damn about the people of those nations. They just want to pay people less because it maximizes profit. And we're supposed to celebrate that?

Bleed employees dry, bleed customers dry, bleed the environment dry, all to maximize revenue at any cost, because for some reason, we're told that's what success is. To every billionaire in the world, I'd like to ask, "What's wrong with making only $500 million? Would it really ruin your life to take $100 million and give it to your employees? Why the hell don't you have a thousand employees making $100,000 a year, instead of hoarding $2 billion for yourself that no reasonable person could ever need?"

Why do we think someone like Michael Bloomberg is a great man? Yeah, he made all of his money from his financial data terminal, but he didn't create the damn thing. A lot of people helped him create the technology and deliver it to customers, but he's the one sitting on billions of dollars. How many people had to bleed so he could sit on his billions? How many people worked harder than him for a lot less money to make him filthy rich?

That's not greatness, and it's not success. It's fucking embarrassing. And if people knew what it really takes to become the next Bloomberg, or Bezos, or Elon Musk, if they knew the full impact of one man accumulating and hoarding billions of dollars, they wouldn't be praising these guys and putting them on magazine covers.

In business school, in the financial media, in books and magazines, we're told that these guys are authorities on business success. These are the people we're supposed to look up to, listen to, learn from, emulate. Bezos is working people to death in his distribution centers for a shamefully low wage under ridiculous restrictions, and we're supposed to admire him as a leader. It's sickening.

The evil shitheads who made OxyContin and ushered in the opioid crisis eventually agreed to an $8 billion settlement, but how many lives have they ruined? They'll pay their settlements over the course of about fifteen years and probably still be one of the wealthiest families in the world by the end of it, even as millions lay dead and dying from the crisis their greed produced. Oh, well, I guess that's just the cost of being a real success in business and in life, right?

I'm reminded of the Coen brothers movie *The Hudsucker Proxy*, where everyone who becomes CEO of a particular toy company ends up jumping out of the office window when the company struggles financially. They only measure success by revenue, income, profit, and net worth, and it has turned them into broken people.

How much is enough? How much are you willing to sacrifice? How much are you willing to lose just to make more money? "Get rich or die trying." So many people subscribe to this idea, and they're broken people who would blithely trade their families, reputations, and lives just for the chance of getting a fat bank account. Why do we normalize this? Why don't we view it as the sickness that it is?

Coddling the Assholes

I know of a certain business leader whose company has very clearly defined brand values, and most of the people in the company do a decent job of embodying those values in everything they do. However, they have one specific team member in one of their service lines who is blatantly selfish and an unrepentant asshole. He ignores data, advice, and the needs of others, and only ever follows his own opinions. He's incredibly insecure and rude, but the guy makes a lot of money.

And because he makes money, leaders treat him like he can do no wrong. They equate money with wisdom, even though there's no direct correlation, so the asshole operates with impunity. The thing is, he's doing damage to their brand, and eventually it's going to catch up with them. He might get away with it for a while, but a damaged reputation always comes crashing down on you like a rogue wave at some point.

Is it really worth sacrificing your brand and your reputation just to try to get a few more transactions in the short term? Is it really worth trashing employee and customer relationships just so a jerk on your team can squeeze a few more bucks out of some poor browbeaten client somewhere?

We shouldn't be okay with this. If there's any part of you that yearns to be a decent human being, you shouldn't tolerate it for one more second. There's a better way to run a company. I've seen it. I'm living it. Believe it or not, you can run a company by focusing entirely on doing right by people, both internally and externally. You can feel happy and fulfilled by being a good citizen, a decent human being, who doesn't sacrifice a reputation, values, or people just to make a little more money a little faster.

Overnight success isn't real. Stop chasing it. At the time of writing, I'm seven years into my business, and we've had gradual but consistent growth. More importantly, I'm enjoying all of this. I think we've created a great environment for our employees.

Chasing overnight success just sets you up to exploit and hurt people. Chasing endless millions and billions of dollars just turns you into a monster who leaves burned-out people in your wake. The growth hacks and shortcuts don't really work anyway. There's a better fucking way.

Chapter Seven Reflections:

▶ The hoarding of wealth is seen as a sign of wisdom and good leadership, rather than the mental and moral sickness that it is. Shouldn't we stop glorifying the hoarding of wealth and unlimited growth at all costs?

▶ Ask yourself, "How much is enough, honestly?"

▶ Robbing your family of time with you is not success but complete failure.

▶ Is it really worth sacrificing your brand and your reputation just to try to get a few more transactions in the short term?

▶ Those who only measure success by revenue, income, profit, and net worth become broken people.

CHAPTER EIGHT

Creative Problem-Solving

Our education system in this country *must* be sorely lacking. Look at how easily people in this society are influenced into believing things that are clearly absurd. During the pandemic, we had thousands of otherwise decent people taking a drug intended to treat parasitic worms in horses to fight Covid, a respiratory disease, because a handful of jerkoffs on social media convinced them that vaccines are dangerous. It's fucking ridiculous.

Why are people so easily duped? Why do they *allow* themselves to be duped? Education must be failing us, because a large number of people in this country are extremely susceptible to incredibly stupid conspiracy theories.

I suffered in school as a kid. As a creative child who struggled within tight constraints, I had a very hard time making it work for me. I learn best through playing and curiosity, and this got me in trouble a lot, because schools are not set up to reward kids for chasing their own curiosity and imagination.

Eleanor Roosevelt said it best: "I think, at a child's birth, if a mother could ask a fairy godmother to endow it with the most useful gift, that gift should be curiosity." She was dead right, but we don't reward curiosity. Many schools aren't teaching people how to direct their curiosity and play as a means of learning. Indeed, straying from the dull methodology and curriculum tends to get students in trouble, so consequently, people don't really learn the skills to discover, discern, and learn.

I think this makes people more susceptible to being duped.

Schools are bad, but workplaces aren't much better. "Here's our SOPs. Do things *this* way. Don't be too curious. Stay in line." Personally, I think curiosity is the secret to happiness. Traveling, seeking, and exploring cures us of ignorance.

As Mark Twain said, "Travel is fatal to prejudice, bigotry and narrow-mindedness, and many of our people need it sorely on these accounts." Have you noticed that a lot of people who fall for incredibly stupid ideas are people who don't really go anywhere? They live insulated lives, don't experience other cultures, and just get their information from a few channels run by unqualified weirdos? It's not coincidental. They're trapped in an echo chamber, listening to a very small demographic of people spouting the same nonsense back and forth at each other.

To be fair, this is what happens when you're a product of a school system whose approach to learning is, "Listen, memorize, repeat." It makes people mentally weak and incapable of knowing how to really learn and maintain an open mind.

Look, I went to a Catholic school run by nuns, and it was a brutally rigid environment. I remember in fourth grade asking my mom, "If these nuns are supposed to be holy, why are they so mean?" This question may have been the first spark of my eventual atheism, but I couldn't help pushing against the "listen, memorize, repeat" approach to education, and my curiosity, my desire to know, to truly know, led to a lot of punishment.

And then I discovered that the same rigid environment, the same resistance to curiosity, exists in the corporate world as much as it does in the schools. Religious dogma gives way to corporate philosophy, but practically speaking, it works pretty much the same way. "Listen, memorize, repeat."

I think it's because our educational system was chiefly set up to prepare people for the kind of factory jobs that were once common in this country. So if you grew up in Baltimore in the seventies, the schools were essentially preparing you for a life of working at places like Bethlehem Steel in nearby Sparrows Point, because that's where most of the locals wound up. In my hometown of Philadelphia, it was a place like the Westinghouse factory between Lester and Essington, or GE in Southwest Philly.

By the time I got to high school, most of those big factories were gone—shut down or outsourced to the third world—and so were the jobs, so my whole generation was learning to work hard, take direction, and do what they're told so they could succeed at factory jobs that no longer existed.

I think this is a problem endemic to our whole educational approach—it's a system designed to prepare young people for a kind of work life that really doesn't exist anymore. Yes, being too curious and playful might be a problem when your job is to set a panel on a conveyor belt and press a button over and over again for a ten-hour shift. On an assembly line, you need everyone to just do their job or the whole line can get fucked up and people can get injured. "Listen, memorize, repeat."

So we've created entire generations where visionaries were stifled and nobody was taught how to really learn, think for themselves, or embrace their curiosity. When one of my employees or a client is confronted with a problem and their response is to come to me, throw their hands up, and say, "I don't know how to do this," it's a bad sign. A very bad sign. It's "listen, memorize, repeat" in action.

Like every human being, they have the innate ability to learn, explore, and research, to try to find a solution or figure out what they don't know. What I want to hear from people is, "I've never done this before, but let me see if I can figure it out," or, "I don't know the answer, but let me see if I can find it." I'll bend over backward to provide help and support if an employee comes to me with that attitude.

When someone comes to me and says, "I don't know how to do this," I reply, "What would you do if you'd locked your keys in your car? Would you throw your hands up and say, 'I don't know how to get my keys?' Or would you practice a little creative problem-solving and try to figure it out?" That's the mindset you have to commit to if you want to develop and feed the curiosity of you and your team.

At the same time, while problem-solving skills are incredibly valuable and rewarding, you shouldn't try to run a company on the mantra of "Promise the client whatever they want, then figure out how to deliver it later." That approach is short-sighted, dishonest, and unsustainable. Plus, it's incredibly unfair to the people on your team who have to figure out how to deliver the impossible thing that you promised to the client just to close the deal.

Feed Your Mind

When I was a younger man, I went to a lecture by a guy named Von Glitschka who runs a design firm in the Pacific Northwest. He's an incredibly talented guy who has designed logos and characters for some well-known companies, including the updated design for the Kool-Aid Man, the new Toucan Sam for Kellogg's, and the logo for Dungeons & Dragons. In the lecture, he talked about his process, and he gave the following advice: "Get out of your comfort zone, feed your mind, read books on topics you don't think you're interested in. If you feed your mind the same things over and over, your creativity and problem-solving will never blossom."

I decided to follow his advice, so on a whim, I started reading the writings of a philosopher named John Dewey, an educational reformer from the early half of the twentieth century. Dewey promoted a pragmatic approach to learning that embraced "learning by doing." As he put it, "Give the pupils something to do, not something to learn; and the doing is of such a nature as to demand thinking; learning naturally results." He also said, "Were all instructors to realize that the quality of mental process, not the production of correct answers, is the measure of educative growth, something hardly less than a revolution in teaching would be worked."[7]

It was the beginning of a commitment on my part to read and learn on a very wide variety of subjects, not just things pertaining directly to my industry or skill set. I stopped attending industry-specific events and networking only with industry-specific people. Instead, I branched out and met people from other industries. I read books that had nothing to do with design or business leadership.

Of course, this wide range of learning serves me very well now that I'm a creative consultant, because I can help clients see things from different perspectives and offer insights to improve and uncomplicate their business that they might never consider on their own. Plus, being well-read makes us more interesting people. Having eclectic tastes in music and books gives us deep reserves of knowledge to draw on for writing, designing, and speaking. When you

7   https://www.johndeweyphilosophy.com/books/democracy_and_ education/Thinking_in_Education.html

push yourself out of your comfort zone, open yourself to new ideas, and broaden your horizons, you gain access to more powerful problem-solving, as I've experienced first-hand.

There is never just one way to solve a problem. When it comes to your business, there's not a single solution, but there is a best practice: *Open yourself to new ideas and new approaches.* Yes, if you want to repeat your success, you need to develop some kind of consistent process, but if you're open-minded, you can discover surprising ways to improve your processes over time.

Too many people treat success like it's an equation: a single mathematical formula that guarantees success (however the hell they define "success"). In reality, a broad mind allows you to see many variables unique to your situation that you might otherwise overlook. Again, you have to set aside the dogma, test the variables, and see what works for you. When you get results, don't get so stuck in the process that delivered it that you don't keep trying to improve it.

Setting Parameters

Certainly, you have to put parameters around your creativity and problem-solving based on what you're trying to achieve and what your brand is all about. Those parameters take an infinite number of potential solutions and identify a specific space in which you're going to operate.

For example, if you're trying to get your keys out of your locked car, you're probably going to set some parameters that include things like, "We're not going to smash the window, crowbar the door open, or do permanent structural damage to the car, because we still need the vehicle to be in good condition after we've gotten the keys."

That doesn't limit creativity, it enables innovation. Parameters will include things like:

- ▶ Who is our target audience?

- ▶ What outcomes do we expect?

- ▶ What is the pain we're trying to solve?

- ► What would success look like?

- ► What are the requirements?

- ► What is appropriate for our brand?

- ► How do our brand values come into play here?

Once you have parameters in place, then you can begin looking at the problem from different perspectives, using an open-minded approach, to explore and be curious about your solution.

Chapter Eight Reflections:

▸ We've created entire generations where vision-aries were stifled and nobody was taught how to really learn, think for themselves, or embrace their curiosity, but every human being has the innate ability—and desire— to learn, explore, and research, to try to find a solution or figure out what they don't know.

▸ Get out of your comfort zone, open yourself and your mind to new experiences all the time. You won't regret it.

▸ Putting parameters around creativity isn't sti-fling. Instead, it enables innovation. Once you have parameters in place, you can look at the problem from different perspectives, using an open-minded approach, to explore and be curi-ous about your solution.

CHAPTER NINE

Build Your Tribe

No matter how great a person you might be, there are haters, takers, and people who don't want you to succeed.

I once worked with a contractor who tried to solicit my clients while he was working with me. I'd given him a free office, considered him a friend, and bent over backward to help him be successful, but then I caught him in the act of trying to steal a client and had to fire him.

Even when I kicked him to the curb, he tried to make it my fault, not his. Sad. But, it was a learning experience, and I started using NDAs and non-solicitation agreements just to cover my butt—as well as add a level of professionalism (and peace of mind) to the company. It's a shame we can't just trust people, or assume that they will do right by us if we do right by them, but that's how it goes. It doesn't pay to be naïve.

I grew up in Philly, and my neighborhood was so densely populated that I could play with a different group of kids every day and never hang out with the same kids twice. Imagine blocks and blocks of tightly packed row houses, and most of the families were Irish Catholic and having babies like crazy.

Occasionally, my mom would catch me hanging out with some group of kids she didn't like. When that happened, she always said the same thing, "Show me your friends, and I'll tell you who you are."

My mom was right to be worried. Some of the bad kids in the neighborhood liked to hang out with me because they thought I was funny, but also because they could convince me to do crazy things, which amused them.

We've all had the experience of being shaped and influenced by the friends we surround ourselves with. It's especially bad in high school and college, but it continues to be true throughout our lives. Friends can bring out your best, or they can bring out your worst. The same goes for coworkers, associates, and employees.

An article in *Harvard Business Review* put it very well: "When thinking about how to develop in our careers, most of us tend to focus on promotions, projects, courses, certifications. We seek out expanded roles, more senior titles, extra money, larger impact. We overlook one very key piece of the learning puzzle: proactively surrounding ourselves with people who will push us to succeed in unexpected ways and, in so doing, build genuinely rich, purposeful lives of growth, excellence, and impact."[8]

8   https://hbr.org/2018/09/
the-key-to-career-growth-surround-yourself-with-people-who-will-push-you

Think about the people you're surrounded with. Do they genuinely want to see you succeed? Do they want you to be happy? When you get a promotion at work, are they excited for you? Jealous of you? Indifferent? As the article says, "Few of us engage in a deliberate, determined search for those wise individuals who, through their inspiration and advice, can literally make us new."

Ironically, the guy who originally sent me that *Harvard Business Review* article was someone I eventually had to kick out of my life (actually, it was the contractor I mentioned at the beginning of the chapter). He was one of those "friends" who shit on me with disguised feedback and advice meant to be helpful, but in reality created self-doubt and insecurity. In hindsight, he clearly hated to see me succeed—a taker who was quick to abuse my generosity and kindness. We've all had people like this in our lives. You can probably think of a few friends, family members, acquaintances, or coworkers who tend to take advantage of you—or worse.

In a work environment, these kinds of people can hurt your business, hurt your clients, and hurt your revenue, and you can't always predict who the takers are going to be. By the time you realize what kind of person you're dealing with, they might already have done quite a bit of damage. You have to be careful.

Pack animals have this figured out. If a dog in a pack is acting in ways that are dangerous to the pack, the other dogs will try to correct him by snarling, nipping at him, and so on. If that doesn't work, eventually they'll turn on him and kill him in order to protect the pack. Humans aren't always as good at this. If someone is hurting you, taking from you, abusing you, or manipulating you, accept that their intentions toward you aren't good and get them out of your company or out of your life.

I'm not suggesting we all become paranoid and start suspecting everyone of taking from us (like the psycho CEO of Better.com who fired 900 employees, amounting to 9 percent of his entire staff, because they were "stealing" from him). I fully believe in giving people the benefit of the doubt, but sometimes you have to trust your gut. If something feels off about a person, you just might be onto something. Listen to that feeling.

To prevent this, use your values to communicate what you care about, and only work with and for people who give a shit about the same stuff as you. If folks don't share your values, then you probably won't want to be associated with them for long.

Root Out Toxic People

Growing up in my Philly neighborhood surrounded by thousands of people, I kept finding myself in bad situations. I didn't learn to be cautious about people or listen to my gut (or I chose to ignore it). I maintained some friendships that really weren't good for me, and they followed me into college and into my career. Three weeks before I moved to Baltimore to continue my career in a brand-new city, I went to a Flyers game with some guys I grew up with, and afterward we visited a couple of bars. We were a tough group, had a bad influence on each other (or a good influence, depending on when and why you asked), and we often got in trouble.

On that particular night, when we bumped into some equally tough hooligans, we got into a brawl. Fists and bottles started flying. Before I knew it, someone flung a bottle across the bar and hit me right in the face. The bottle broke, my face broke, and blood began to flow. That led to an ambulance ride and stitches.

I remember lying there in the ambulance and hearing my mom's voice in my head.

"Show me your friends, and I'll tell you who you are."

Three weeks later, I started my new job with stitches in my face, but it could have been a hell of a lot worse. At least I hadn't lost any teeth or an eye. Still, it was an embarrassing first impression to make at my new job, and I knew I had to sever ties with my old tribe for good.

I started surrounding myself with people who wanted to see me do well. People who built me up instead of trying to bring me down. It took time, but eventually I created a new tribe for myself, and it transformed my life. Fortunately, I was ninety miles away from a lot of the bad influences, which made cutting ties easier. As I learned that year, the people you're around every day make a much bigger impact on you than you realize. And when you think about your reputation, keep asking yourself, "Are these people helping or hurting?"

Look, there are a lot of crappy people in the world. Some of them are hurting, and they want to see other people hurt. Some just enjoy inflicting pain. I was born in a neighborhood with a lot of guys like that, and I grew up around them. At times, maybe I was just like them. But if I'd stayed, there would have been no maybe. Fortunately, I got out.

You have to get the toxic people out of your life. WebMD defines a toxic person as "anyone whose behavior adds negativity and upset to your life," and identifies the following warning signs:

- You feel like you're being manipulated into something you don't want to do.

- You're constantly confused by the person's behavior.

- You feel like you deserve an apology that never comes.

- You always have to defend yourself to this person.

- You never feel fully comfortable around them.

- You continually feel bad about yourself in their presence.[9]

Toxic people make you worse. Is there a person in your life who is jealous, aggressive, or manipulative? If you don't get away from them, they'll hurt you, and they'll influence you to hurt others. Get them out of your life. Surround yourself with people who care for

9   https://www.webmd.com/mental-health/signs-toxic-person

you, appreciate you, and build you up, and let them inspire you to do the same. And remember those micro-managers we talked about earlier? They're toxic—toxic to your people, your company, and even you.

In business, put together a team of people who are real teammates, people you can coordinate with, who share the same goals, and who don't resent contributing to the success of others. People who want to see you happy, fulfilled, and excited. Then make sure you are that kind of teammate for them as well.

I think about my parents. They have always wanted me to succeed. I almost dropped out of college after the first year. I'm glad I didn't, but after three years, I had an epiphany and wanted to go to art school. I skipped a semester, then transferred to another school. I changed my major from science to animation. I was trying to find my way, and I made some risky decisions, but my parents had my back through all of it. They supported me and encouraged me, because they wanted me to be happy and pursue a life I would be excited about and enjoy.

When I started my own agency, I faced many challenges and took on a huge amount of risk. It was a dangerous endeavor for my family, because I was putting our financial future on the line, and I almost worked myself to death to get the business off the ground. By the time my second child was born, we were practically broke because I'd poured everything into the agency. Propr has always been profitable, but the early years were a bit tight while my wife was at home with the kids and we were living on a single salary.

My wife's parents helped support us through that period of time because they really wanted to see us succeed. Eventually things turned around, and the company started turning larger profits, but I don't think we would have gotten to that point without the support of my in-laws.

So I've seen firsthand the impact of being surrounded by toxic people, *and* I've seen the impact of being surrounded by supportive people. And I can say unequivocally, it makes all the difference in the world. I encourage you to be very deliberate about getting the toxic people out of your company and out of your life!

That's not always easy to do. Sadly, even though I found better friends in Baltimore, the job that brought me there turned out to be a shitty environment with toxic leaders who treated me so badly that on the weekends, when I would hang out with my friends, I couldn't enjoy myself. The bad feelings from work chased me into Saturday night. But I couldn't leave the job because I needed the money.

When you find yourself in a predicament like that, even if you can't leave, you can begin working intentionally toward getting out of it. In regard to your business, you can avoid this predicament in the first place if you're very careful about who you hire. First of all, make sure you hire people based on their experience and alignment with your core values, not where they went to school, or their connections, or some other superficial factor.

And for fuck's sake, don't hire your cousin, your sister, or some other family member. Nepotism is almost always a complete disaster. Family members can—and often will—use their connection to you as a way to exploit other employees or shirk responsibility.

Make sure you're not a toxic person yourself. You know the old saying: "If you run into an asshole in the morning, you ran into an asshole. If you run into assholes all day, *you're* the asshole."

Personally, I genuinely want to take care of my family and my team. I want to help clients create their own awesome stories of success. I want to help improve lives, empower people, and enable them to achieve greatness, while minimizing as much bullshit as possible. These are the things that matter most to me—far more than just making money—and I'm determined to surround myself with people who are driven by the same passion. I have no interest in making millions of dollars if people have to suffer for it. If my team is making my company profitable, but they hate my guts, then I consider that a total failure.

Surround yourself with the right people. It's as simple as that. Find people who share your values and give a shit, who will work enthusiastically because they believe in what you're doing, they give a shit about the same stuff you give a shit about, and want to see you succeed.

As that *Harvard Business Review* article concludes, "Proactively seeking out and cultivating those who will help us become better versions of ourselves is, by a wide margin, the key for living a truly happy and meaningful life."

I couldn't agree more. And by the way, one of the people who should be helping you become a better, healthier, happier version of yourself is *you!*

Chapter Nine Reflections:

▶ Friends can bring out your best, or they can bring out your worst. The same goes for coworkers, associates, and employees.

▶ "Few of us engage in a deliberate, determined search for those wise individuals who, through their inspiration and advice, can literally make us new."

▶ Use your values to communicate what you care about, and work for/with only those who give a shit about the same stuff you give a shit about. If folks don't share your values, then likely you won't want to be associated with them for very long.

▶ If someone is hurting you, taking from you, abusing you, or manipulating you, accept that their intentions toward you aren't good and get

them out of your company or out of your life.
Surround yourself with people who care for you,
appreciate you, and build you up, and let them
inspire you to do the same.

CHAPTER TEN

Take Care of Yourself

So why the hell do we only measure success by one metric: money? Why is that the single defining factor that determines whether or not we've "made it?" Yes, you might have accrued a lot of money, and your company might be profitable, but what was the cost to your family? What was the cost to your health and your mental and emotional well-being? What was the cost to your team, customers, and the world? Is it possible that you paid a higher price to acquire that money than it was worth?

When we talk to clients, we often begin by encouraging them to develop a clear long-term vision for their company and their own career success. Often, they default to setting a purely financial goal. "I want to make $100 million dollars over the course of my career." But is it really worth making $100 million over the course of your career if it means you won't be around to watch your kids grow up and your employees won't be around to watch their own kids grow up?

You might get to that goal a lot faster if you overwork people, overwork yourself, pay employees as little as possible, and slash expenses to such a degree that working at your company is a bare-bones, hellish experience, but then what? Will you enjoy clinging to that pile of money as you walk right into an early grave, with no relationships with your adult children and a debris field of miserable lives in your wake?

But why should that be your goal in the first place? What about carefully building and cultivating a brand (remember, your brand *is* your reputation) that you can be proud of? What about taking care of your employees and customers? What about just giving a shit?

Here's a wild idea. Set long-term goals for your company that include things like 1) how you're going to take care of people, 2) how much you're going to pay employees, 3) the way your company is going to embody your values and make an impact, 4) how you're going to achieve financial success in a way that you can feel proud of. You'll still probably be able to retire and play a shit-ton of golf, but at least you and others will feel good about your career accomplishments. At least your kids might come to visit you from time to time because they like you, not just to keep their names on your will. At least your employees will remember you fondly and be better off for having worked with you.

Consider your personal goals. There has to be more to life than working to make more money. Wouldn't you like to be able to spend some time with your kids and friends on a regular basis? Wouldn't it be nice if you could drop your kids off at school in the morning and have those few minutes to talk to them? Wouldn't it be nice to devote a significant amount of time to your physical, mental, and emotional health?

So many business leaders need to do a much better job at taking care of themselves. If you would commit to taking care of your health and well-being, I guarantee your company would be a lot better for it. Your family would be better for it. And you would get to actually enjoy the wealth that you acquire.

Fucking Pay People What They're Worth!

I told this story earlier, but it's worth repeating. Way back in 1999, I got my first industry job working for a company in southern Jersey that paid me $40,000 a year. At that time, it was a pretty sweet salary. Twenty dollars an hour is amazing when minimum wage is only $6. Unfortunately, when the tech bubble burst, that company went bust, and the nice salary went with it.

My next job was at a much larger company that paid me $33,000 a year. I lost a quarter of my income for a job that was a hell of a lot more painful. The company always told employees that their performance would lead to a raise, but my annual raise was never more than about 4 percent. When I mentioned the decrease in salary at performance reviews, they always said the same thing: "Don't worry. You'll get there."

Despite the shitty pay, I consistently exceeded expectations, excelled at performance reviews, and wound up getting promoted into management. However, they just wouldn't give me a significant raise. Their entire sales team made about $20,000 a year *more* than me, plus incentives, which told me something about how much they valued the work I was doing.

I felt a little like the cart horse in *Animal Farm*. If you've read the book, you remember Boxer, the cart horse who believes any problem will be solved if he just works harder. The pigs who run the farm keep promising the horse that he will be rewarded for all of his hard work, but it never happens. Eventually,

Boxer works himself to death, and gets sent off to the glue factory.

That's how I felt. After four years of hard work, exceeding expectations, and a promotion, I never got close to my previous salary, even as company executives, the sales team, and many others were raking in big bucks. The message was clear. My contribution wasn't valued, and they just didn't care to pay me what I was worth. They wanted to use me up until I had nothing more to give and then they could send me off to the proverbial glue factory.

So I did the only reasonable thing I could do: I accepted a better position at another company as soon as it came along. Just before I left, I attended a corporate dinner at Texas Roadhouse, and the company owner waved me over.

"Hey, I hear you're leaving us," he said.

Trying to be a professional, I replied, "Yeah, that's true, but this has been a great experience, and I appreciate it."

And his response?

He shrugged, said, "Oh, well," and that was it.

Now, bear in mind, I'd built an entire department for that company, and we were making them a lot of money. I poured my blood, sweat, and tears into the company for less money than I deserved, and all I got when I left was an, "Oh, well." Clearly, that's all I was worth to them.

I'm not sharing this to engender sympathy for my career hardships. I'm sharing it because I know there are a hell of a lot of underpaid, underappreciated people out there busting their asses for companies who don't see the value of their contributions. Some of them might even be working for your company. Some of them might even be you.

Health benefits, retirement accounts, and paid time-off are nice, but they're often used as leverage to underpay workers. "I have to keep working for this company because I don't want to lose my benefits. If I work for myself, I'll have no health insurance." It's a trap that keeps people in toxic work environments longer than they want to be there. And, by the way, time off isn't a *reward* for good work; it's a *requirement* for people to deliver their best work.

For too long, we've been told that hard work is the secret to wealth. If that was true, day laborers and construction workers would be filthy rich, instead of being among the lowest-paid professionals. The truth is, a lot of people work hard and never get paid what they deserve. Actually, the only real guaranteed path to wealth is to be born into it, so if you really want to take care of yourself, don't sacrifice your happiness, wellness, or health for someone who doesn't appreciate it.

Fortunately, there's been a massive shift in what young workers will put up with. These days, younger people are refusing to take jobs, or hold onto jobs, where they are underpaid and overworked. They've seen previous generations of workers being exploited, and they're not willing to tolerate it or accept it as normal. They've seen companies making CFOs into CEOs because they only care about lining their own pockets. They've seen companies outsourcing their entire operations to third-world countries, laying off tens of thousands of people so they can pay slave wages overseas.

They've seen big factories like Bethlehem Steel shut down, turning out their entire workforce, even as the guy who acquired the assets of the company and bankrupted the pension fund, Wilbur Ross (who some say was the inspiration for Monty Burns on *The Simpsons*) continues to sit on a mountain of money. Wilbur Ross was the secretary of commerce under Trump, and that fucker took money from the people who worked at Bethlehem Steel, people that were close to retirement, and people who were living off pensions, even though he was already a billionaire. The younger generation has seen this kind of shit, and they're less willing to participate in it on any level.

Making Someone Else's Dreams Come True

So, what about the people who work for you? Are they underpaid and underappreciated? Are you okay knowing that they hate coming to work, resent how little they're paid, and fucking hate you? Are you really okay with it?

If you're breeding resentment everywhere you go, you're not taking care of your people, and just as importantly, you're not taking care of yourself. When you hire someone, you're asking them to go to battle with you, but if you really want them to commit, they have to fully buy into your vision. They have to believe in what you're doing, and how they're contributing to it.

Nobody is going to be highly motivated or super passionate if they think their hard work is just making you rich. One advantage of starting my own company is that I was no longer busting my ass just to make someone else's dreams come true. Ideally, everyone's dreams are coming true to some extent in a company, right?

I was walking to a restaurant up the street one evening when I saw a commotion around the front of a CVS store. A guy came flying out of the door carrying two large jugs of laundry detergent. As he took off down a nearby alley, a CVS employee chased after him.

I shouted at the employee, "Dude, what are you doing? Why are you risking your life, your health, and your future just to get a couple bottles of laundry detergent back from a shoplifter? Let him go! That company doesn't give a shit about you. If you get hurt or die they'll just replace you. That dude just needs to do his laundry."

The employee stopped chasing the guy and turned around. He looked at me and said, "You're right," and went back inside the store.

We think we're supposed to sacrifice everything to the company. Give it your all! That's why we have people working ridiculous amounts of overtime when they're only paid a nine-to-five salary.

The last agency I worked for before starting my own business just expected everyone to work over-time constantly. In company meetings, leaders said things like, "Work hard, play harder," and talked about work/life balance, and all of that bullshit, but they got annoyed when people went home at five o'clock. I remember the owners of the company complaining, "Why aren't there more people working here late at night?"

The answer that no one dared to say was, "Because you pay us to work from nine to five, asshole. We want to fucking go home!"

Why are so many company leaders comfortable using people up? I'm so glad fewer and fewer young workers are willing to put up with it. They know they have choices. More than that, they know damn well it doesn't have to be that way. Employees deserve to feel happy, fulfilled, engaged, and healthy when they work for a company just as much as the owners. All of us—owners, leaders, and employees—should be able to care of ourselves and live a good life.

Taking Care of Yourself

Taking care of yourself is about more than your salary, of course. It's also about your health. I consider myself fortunate that I come from a family that instilled the values of exercise and healthy living. My father was a powerlifter and had a box full of trophies, and I have a memory of watching my aunt run a 5k race in downtown Philly when I was little.

I've completed marathons, ultramarathons, and triathlons, and a slew of other fitness endeavors. While I enjoy the challenges, I hope all of those activities are contributing to a legacy for my kids so they will take care of themselves as well. When I moved to Fells Point, Baltimore, the local bars soon became my natural habitat. Before long, I met and began dating my wife, and we spent a lot of time on the weekends hanging out at the bars in Fells Point, drinking beer, socializing, and having fun.

Later that year, during a routine checkup, my doctor, a real piece of work named Vincenzo, said in this thick Italian accent, "What are you doing to take care of yourself? Are you exercising?"

And I replied, "Ah, Doc, I used to, but I don't have any time now. "

"Ah, Bob, there's always time for exercise," he said.

That simple statement stuck with me, and it changed my life. If you want to take care of yourself, you gotta get out there and *make the time*, and if it's important to you, then you will find the time, no matter how many other responsibilities you have to juggle.

When you're spending your whole life at work, you are risking absolutely everything in your life. So you work nights and weekends, you work when you're on vacation, and what's the reward? Whatever you think the reward is, chances are it's not worth the sacrifice, especially if you're working for someone else.

At some companies, a lot of good productive time is wasted in meetings, so people are forced to come in early and stay late to get work done. Similarly, many leaders fail to set healthy boundaries because they think the company needs their full attention every moment of every day in order to survive.

Can you imagine if you started dating someone and you had absolutely no boundaries in place from the beginning? They could text you or call you in the middle of the night. They could show up at your home or at work at any time and interrupt what you're doing. It would be a fucking nightmare.

Healthy relationships need boundaries. Nobody can or should be instantly available all the time. It's okay to tell that person you're dating, "Hey, I'm hanging out with my friends tonight. We can get together tomorrow." And if it's not okay, then you're probably in a toxic relationship with a jealous, controlling asshole.

Well, the same goes for work. Technology has made it possible to get in contact with just about anyone at any time, but that shouldn't obligate people to be available at any time. Personally, my phone doesn't notify me about anything from 8pm to 8am. I put the phone down in the evening, and I don't look at it again until morning.

In my last job, I would get home late every night and have about twenty minutes to see my daughter before she went to sleep. Usually, she was already in bed, and she was cranky and tired. So it wasn't even quality time. I was robbing her of the better time that she deserved as my kid, and for what?

Fortunately, now that I own my career and my future, I get to see my kids as much as I want, and I've created a culture in which my employees have the same privilege. And it *is* a privilege. With the way we do business in today's world, it is still a privilege, but it should be the norm.

I give my people plenty of time off because I want them to be refreshed and recharged. We shut down the company for almost two weeks during the winter holidays, and we offer plenty of time off throughout the year. What I want for myself, I want for them as well: time to spend with loved ones, to be healthy, to have a life outside of work. To reiterate: Time off shouldn't be treated as a reward for good work. Rather, it should be seen as a necessity for great work.

Being healthy, spending time with your kids, taking care of yourself, and not working yourself to death should all be the norm, because *not* doing so is fucking *abnormal*!

Chapter Ten Reflections:

▶ Set long-term goals for your company that include things like 1) how you're going to take care of people, 2) how much you're going to pay employees, 3) the way your company is going to embody your values and make an impact, and 4) how you're going to achieve financial success in a way that you can feel proud of.

▶ If you're breeding resentment everywhere you go, you're not taking care of your people, and just as importantly, you're not taking care of yourself.

▶ Being healthy, spending time with your kids, taking care of yourself, and not working yourself to death should all be the norm, because not doing so is fucking abnormal!

- ► Nobody is going to be highly motivated or super passionate if they think their hard work is just making you rich.

- ► Time off isn't a reward for good work, it's a necessity for *great* work.

CONCLUSION

So, what does it all come down to? A simple message really. If you care about your brand, then you should build it the right way. That means helping, not hurting. That means contributing and giving, not just taking. And how you do that is starting with your core values. As you grow your business, remember why you did it in the first place, and remember the people who have helped and contributed along the way. Give credit generously, take the blame, and seek constant improvement.

In other words, be a decent human being.

You know where you came from, but that doesn't define you. What defines you is the vision you're working toward, and the journey you take to get there. Consider carefully the people who accompany you on that journey.

When I worked for that large beer wholesaler in Philly, I made some great relationships, even though working for the company was like *Animal Farm*. I was a wild-west Philly dude back in those days, which means I kept it really raw. But it also means I made real relationships with people. Even though I left that company fifteen years ago, I still talk to some of my coworkers from those days.

In fact, I chatted with a guy from those days recently, and I learned that he's now the president of a brewery in New Jersey, and he'd been thinking about hiring my firm. (He has since hired us, and we are working together). It's amazing how a relationship from a four-year job that I left fifteen years ago has remained so strong that this guy still thought of me and reached out when he needed help.

He's worked with other agencies, and he knows all sorts of creative people. But the authenticity of the relationship we built when we worked on the same team lingered in his mind all these years later. He knows I will help him and not hurt him, I will give generously and not just take. That's the strength of the relationship we built, even though we were both working for the pigs in *Animal Farm* at the time.

Do Something About It

I met with a B2B client recently to talk to them about repositioning and rebranding his company. He lacked a strong brand identity, because they branded all of their products and services, which created brand confusion and very little brand equity. Quite frankly, they needed a new name.

It's always a touchy conversation when I tell a client, "You need to change your name." There tends to be an emotional connection and history to the existing name, so I approach it very carefully. I scheduled a meeting and prepared to have this conversation with the client, bracing myself for pushback.

Fortunately, we had been building a relationship with the company by providing value, so I felt like I'd won the right to broach the subject. We put together some visuals to justify this recommendation, but before we had the chance to present it to the owner, he spoke up and said, "No one knows us by the name of our company. They know us by the name of our SaaS product. I think we need to change our name."

As it turned out, we had already helped him come to the conclusion. It's usually very contentious when you tell an established fifteen-year-old company to change their name, but this guy was already thinking about it. That told me he clearly trusted us, because we had been delivering a lot of value, and through that value we'd developed a relationship.

I admire the guy because he was willing to set his pride aside and make a big change for the sake of creating a stronger and more meaningful brand. It's easy to complain about what's wrong, but making those big changes takes a lot of guts. There's a lot wrong with the way companies do business today. We all know it. There are a hell of a lot of problems, and plenty of people complain about them. Taking steps to make real, meaningful change takes courage.

In the song "Plateau" by the Meat Puppets there's a lyric that says, "Who needs action when we got words?" Plenty of people talk about what's wrong. They post about. They sit around bitching to each other. That's easy.

After quitting a toxic agency once upon a time, I continued hanging out with some of the people who still worked there. All they did was complain constantly about their boss. Finally, during happy hour at a bar one day, I told them, "I don't think I want to hang out with you guys anymore. All you do is complain, but what are you doing to change things? What are you doing to fix it? If it's impossible to fix the company, then what are you going to do to fix *your* situation? Don't just complain; do something about it."

And I got up and left.

It's like people who complain about the government but don't vote. It's like big brands posting about social ills on social media. Does Kellogg's really support Black Lives Matter or Pride Month or refugees just because they make Twitter posts about it? This kind of virtue signalling is meaningless, embarrassing, and revolting. There are far too many people bitching about problems without actually making any concrete difference. They'll put a sign in their yard, but they won't do shit to fix it.

If you want to make a difference for your company, for the culture, for your department, for your team, your customers, your family, yourself, then start working toward improvement. Make changes for the better! Change your brand, and if you can't change your brand, then change your situation. But do something!

Maybe you're really struggling right now. You're in a shitty work environment, either as the boss or as an employee, but you can start pouring energy into making things better. If you're the boss, then I want you to hear me loud and clear. You *can* change the way you run your business. You don't have to be cutthroat or a manipulator or an exploiter of your people. It is possible to achieve success without hurting people, or hurting yourself.

You can share success with your team, take care of your family and friends, and make a positive impact on your community. It's possible, because there are people doing it right now.

You can be wildly successful *and* a decent human being. Actually, let me put it another way. You can be wildly successful *because* you're a decent human being.

Build your brand like you give a shit, and you'll leave a legacy that you, your kids, your friends, and your coworkers will be proud of.

Tool and Resource for Building Your Brand

I've put together some free tools and resources to help you build your brand in a better way, including templates, worksheets, articles, and podcasts on a variety of relevant topics. Head over to proprdesign.com to check them out.

ACKNOWLEDGEMENTS

To my parents, thanks for encouraging and fostering my creative mind.

To my wife and children, thanks for believing in and dealing with me.

To my sister and brother, this rat would be nothing special if it wasn't for you two.

To my Propr Team, thanks for taking care of business and allowing me the flexibility to pursue this endeavor.

To Jeffrey Miller, thanks for managing me through this process.

And to Michael Zipursky, thanks for inspiring me to take this imperfect strategic action.

I am truly grateful.

ABOUT THE AUTHOR

Bobby Gillespie advises B2B tech brands on scaling through holistic strategies and creative work; he founded Propr Design in 2014—the muscle behind his advising—a Baltimore-based B2B brand growth consultancy and creative agency. Born and raised in Philadelphia, he lives in Baltimore with his wife, kids, and dogs.

CPSIA information can be obtained
at www.ICGtesting.com
Printed in the USA
BVHW031524151222
654222BV00013B/1680

9 798218 032609